English for Academic Research

Series Editor

Adrian Wallwork
English for Academics SAS
Pisa, Italy

This series aims to help non-native English-speaking researchers communicate in English. The books in this series are designed like manuals or user guides to help readers find relevant information quickly, and assimilate it rapidly and effectively. The author has divided each book into short subsections of short paragraphs with many bullet points.

More information about this series at http://www.springer.com/series/13913

Adrian Wallwork

English for Academic CVs, Resumes, and Online Profiles

 Springer

Adrian Wallwork
English for Academics SAS
Pisa, Italy

ISSN 2625-3445 ISSN 2625-3453 (electronic)
English for Academic Research
ISBN 978-3-030-11089-5 ISBN 978-3-030-11090-1 (eBook)
https://doi.org/10.1007/978-3-030-11090-1

This Springer imprint is published by the registered company Springer Nature Switzerland AG
The registered company address is: Gewerbestrasse 11, 6330 Cham, Switzerland

Introduction

Who is this book for?

The book is intended for both native and non-native speakers of English. It focuses mainly on graduates and PhD students, and also young people who are already in employment and are looking for a new job. It is intended primarily for those working in academia and research.

Many of the principles outlined in this book are also relevant for business. In fact, some parts of the book were based on *CVs, Resumes, and LinkedIn*, which is part of the *A Guide to Professional English* series published by Springer.

How is this book organized?

The first two chapters discuss:

- the quality of a good CV or resume
- how recruiters and HR people make their judgments
- whether using a template is a good idea

Chapters 3 and 4 outline what to write at the top of the CV—personal details and short profile. Chapter 4 also discusses how to write an online profile / biography.

Chapters 5-9 examine the other main sections of a CV:

- education
- work experience
- skills (technical and soft)
- personal interests

Chapters 10 and 11 regard how to get a reference, and how to write a reference letter and a cover letter.

The final chapter (Chapter 12) details which elements of your English you will need to check before sending off your CV.

In the appendix is a template for a CV. This template can also be downloaded here: https://e4ac.com/courses-downloads/

How are the chapters organized?

Each chapter has the following four-part format:

1) FACTOIDS

This section contain factoids (i.e. interesting facts and figures) that introduce the topic of the chapter. They can also be used by EAP teachers as warm-ups for lessons. All the statistics and quotations are genuine, though in some cases I have been unable to verify the original source. Note: a few of the statistics are 'recycled' from other books in this series.

2) WHAT'S THE BUZZ?

This is designed to get readers thinking about the topic, through a variety of exercises. These exercises can be done either by the reader alone, or in class with an EAP (English for Academic Purposes) teacher / trainer. The final part of each *What's the buzz?* section is a brief outline of the contents of the chapter. The keys to some of the exercises are contained at the end of the book. If you are a teacher and enjoy these *What's the buzz?* exercises you can find many more in my self published series of *Discussion* books (see 'Other Books'—the penultimate subsection of this Introduction).

3) The main part of each chapter is divided up into short subsections discussing specific issues. The subsections are in the form of frequently asked questions (FAQs) with answers.

4) Each chapter ends with a summary and / or a list of do's and don'ts.

How should I read this book?

This book is designed to be like a manual or a user guide—you don't need to read it starting from page one. Like a manual it has lots of short subsections and is divided into short paragraphs with many bullet points. This is to help you find what you want quickly and also to assimilate the information as rapidly and as effectively as possible.

You can use the Table of Contents as a checklist of things to remember.

I am a trainer in EAP and EFL. Should I read this book? Can I use it as a CV course book?

If you are a teacher of English for Academic Purposes or English as a Foreign Language you will learn about all the typical problems that non-native students have when writing a CV.

The book can be used as the basis of a course on writing CVs / resumes. You will find opportunities for generating a lot of stimulating and fun discussions by using the factoids and the *What's the buzz?* exercises.

If you are interested in other aspects of Academic English, then you can read the teacher's book which contains notes on how to exploit the other books in the series: *English for Academic Research: A Guide for Teachers.*

Is this a book of guidelines or a book of rules?

Guidelines, not rules.

The book is based on interviews with recruiters and HR managers, and an analysis of hundreds of CVs from around 40 different countries.

The result is a series of guidelines on how I think a good CV and cover letter should look, not objective rules. Inevitably, you may not agree with all the suggestions, and are thus totally free to ignore them.

Terminology used in this book

CV (also written *curriculum vitae*)

A reverse chronology listing your education, work experience, skills and interests. Generally two pages long, and typically used in all Anglo countries apart from the US and Canada.

Resume (also written *résumé*)

A brief summary of your achievements and skills, not necessarily in reverse chronological order, and generally not as comprehensive as a CV. Generally one page long, and typically used in the US and Canada.

Recruiter

Someone who works for an agency that finds potential candidates, whose CVs and resumes are then submitted to the agency's clients.

Human resources (HR) manager

> The person in an organization who deals with staff in general, and specifically recruitment and employment.

Hiring manager

> The person responsible for deciding whom to employ.

For the sake of simplicity, although a CV and resume are not exactly the same, I will generally just use the term CV. And although a recruiter, HR manager and hiring manager do different jobs, I will often use these terms indiscriminately.

How dates are used in this book

CVs are full of dates of when you started and finished an activity. For the purposes of this book, I am imagining that we are now in 2030. So unless you are reading this book in 2030, most dates will appear to be in the future.

Examples used in this book

All the examples used in this book have been taken from real CVs, cover letters, reference letters, etc. The only things that have been changed are personal details, dates and layout / font.

I use *he* or *she* at random to refer to the candidate who produced the CV or cover letter.

Other books in this series

This book is a part of series of books to help non-native English-speaking researchers to communicate in English. Other titles that you might like to read are:

English for Writing Research Papers

English for Research: Usage, Style, and Grammar

English for Presentations at International Conferences

English for Academic Research: Grammar / Vocabulary / Writing Exercises

English for Academic Correspondence

English for Interacting on Campus

English for Academic Research: Typical Mistakes

You can find a description of the books plus sample downloads here:

https://www.springer.com/series/13913

For EFL / ESL teachers: Other books you might find interesting.

Easy English: typical grammar and vocabulary mistakes; language games, personality tests, wordsearches, jokes. Details at: https://www.springer.com/series/15586

Guides to Professional English: CVs, presentations, meetings, negotiations, technical manuals, and socializing. Details at: https://www.springer.com/series/13345

Discussions AZ and other discussion books. Details at: https://e4ac.com/teacher-resource-books/

Acknowledgements

Big thanks to Anna Southern and Philippa Holme for editing the original version of this book. Also, thanks to my students, fellow teachers, friends and family who kindly allowed me to use extracts from their CVs, cover letters, personal statements, reference letters, etc.

Special thanks to: Joanna Andronikou, Celine Angbeletchy, Kamran Baheri, Matteo Borzoni, Lisa Caturegli, Chengcheng Yang, Matthew Fletcher, Yohannes Gedamu Gebre, Sara Macchi, Lena dal Pozzo, Giacomo Porzio, Bui Thanh Liem, Hayley Wallwork, Stuart Wallwork, Sharon Zeller.

Thanks to these two great profs: Dan Grossman for letting me use his profile, and Jonathan Birch for his permission to use a Facebook post.

I would also like to thank Philippe Tissot for allowing me to include extracts from the Europass template (http://europass.cedefop.europa.eu/en/home).

The author

Adrian Wallwork is the co-founder of English for Academics (e4ac.com), which specializes in editing and revising scientific papers, as well as teaching English as a foreign language to PhD students. He is the author of over 30 textbooks for Springer Science+Business Media, Cambridge University Press, Oxford University Press, the BBC, and many other publishers. In 2019 he began marketing his self-published *Discussion* books for EFL teachers and students.

Contents

Chapter 1
Preliminaries - thinking about the type of job you want

Factoids

❖ A UK study found that 2 in 5 people in professional jobs are unhappy, partly because of boredom, fatigue or anger. The industries most affected by low job satisfaction were marketing, legal, hospitality, accounting and computing.

❖ Recruiters and HR staffing personnel receive 100-400+ resumes a day if they have posted a job on the open market.

❖ A survey of over 300 UK employers revealed that 50% of recruiters felt that a logical order in the presentation was the most important thing to consider on a CV. 91% of recruiters see a Word document of two to three pages as the best option for a CV.

❖ In 2002, a survey found that 30 seconds is average time spent by recruiter to read a CV. Today the time is around 5-6 seconds.

❖ A survey conducted by UK Job Forecast found that the majority of HR people use the web as part of their strategy and will screen candidates by checking any information about them on personal websites, LinkedIn, Facebook, Twitter etc. Over 60% of employers questioned by CareerBuilder.com rejected candidates on the basis of information that their recruiters had discovered online.

❖ Research shows that despite the effort selectors and candidates put into interviews, they are actually rather a fallible tool for measuring future performance - past performance provides a more accurate measure.

❖ Employers routinely get thousands of CVs from candidates seeking the same job, i.e. a candidate may only have a 1 in 1000 chance of getting an interview. A well thought-out CV can boost a candidate's chances of being interviewed to 1 in 3.

❖ The result of many interviews may be decided by interviewers within the first two or three minutes. These decisions are often made at an intuitive level in relation to the rapport that between interviewer and interviewee.

© Springer Nature Switzerland AG 2019
A. Wallwork, *English for Academic CVs, Resumes, and Online Profiles*,
English for Academic Research, https://doi.org/10.1007/978-3-030-11090-1_1

1.1 What's the buzz?

A) Decide which of these statements are myths (i.e. often believed but not true in reality).

1. The main aim of your CV is to persuade an employer to offer you an interview.

2. You need to exaggerate your skills and experience in order to attract the best jobs.

3. You need to have had lots of experience in order to get a job.

4. Your CV has to be at least two pages long.

5. Your CV should be contain many adjectives designed to highlight your skills and impress the reader.

6. The information that you provide must be quantifiable.

7. Your CV is likely to be scanned, so key words are of paramount importance.

B) How would you answer the following questions?

- Am I more interested in a career where I can use my skills or one which will satisfy my interests?

- How would I describe myself in one sentence?

- What are my greatest skills and how might they match the job I am looking for?

- What are my major accomplishments? How might these be relevant for a particular job?

- Do I like working independently or as part of a team? Would I make a good team leader?

- Do I mind (enjoy) working long hours? How well do I deal with deadlines?

- What are the most important factors I am looking for in my ideal job?

Your answers to these questions should help you first decide what kind of job you would like, and secondly to decide the content of your CV.

C) Below are 20 typical questions asked in interviews. Choose 10 questions and then discuss how you would answer them.

1. Why did you decide to continue in research rather than go into industry?

2. How did you choose the university you attended and why did you pick your particular degree?

1.1 What's the buzz? (cont.)

3. Would you choose the same course again?

4. Apart from what you have learned from an academic point of view, what other skills have you learned from being at university?

5. What parts of your course did you find the most interesting / difficult

6. What contribution did you make to tutorials, seminars, and workshops?

7. How do you prepare for examinations?

8. What obstacles did you face during your time at university?

9. What personal qualities did university help you to develop?

10. What would your supervisor / professor say about your strengths and weaknesses? How would your fellow students judge you?

11. How do you cope with deadlines? What type of deadlines have you had to deal with?

12. What teaching experience have you had?

13. How did you cope when papers were rejected or experiments did not produce the expected results?

14. What is your greatest achievement so far / to date?

15. What kind of team member are you?

16. What was the most satisfying aspect of writing your thesis / dissertation?

17. What do you think are the differences between a job in research and a job in industry?

18. Have your research interests / career interests changed much over the last few years?

19. What difficulties did you encounter with your professor / supervisor? How did you deal with them?

20. Given that English is not your first language, how would you cope with a job outside your country?

D) For an ironic perspective on writing CVs, see the Polish poet Wisława Szymborska-Włodek's poem 'Writing a Curriculum Vitae' - just type in her name and the title of her poem into your search engine.

1.1 What's the buzz? (cont.)

This chapter focuses on the purpose of a CV and helps you to analyse the type of job you want. You will learn what research institutes and companies are really looking for. You are advised to always be honest, to be aware that recruiters will cross check your CV with your Facebook, LinkedIn and other profiles, and that sending the same CV to several companies / institutes is not a good approach.

Note: Unless otherwise stated, the terms *CV* and *resume* are used interchangeably in this chapter.

1.2 What is the purpose of a CV / resume?

The aim of your CV or resume is to encourage a recruiter to contact you regarding a possible job.

Write your CV from the point of view of the person who will read it, i.e. a recruiter in an agency, an HR person in a company or research institute, a professor or fellow researcher in a research team.

This means you should:

- use a format that will be familiar to the reader (i.e. a standard template, which you can modify where appropriate) rather than a format that you have designed totally by yourself. A standard format is easier to navigate for the reader - he / she knows exactly where to look in order to find what he / she is interested in

- only include details that are relevant to the job you are looking for

- clearly highlight your skills and qualifications

- be honest and accurate, and as objective as possible

A CV is thus not an opportunity for you to:

- write every single detail of your career history, education history and personal history

- experiment with your design skills

1.3   What are research institutes really looking for? And companies?

Both research institutes and companies want to see evidence on your CV that you are qualified in terms of both education and work experience for the position that they have open. But they also want evidence that you:

- have a strong work ethic and that you work to deadlines

- can work in a team

- are both proactive and flexible

- have the technical, emotional and analytical skills for problem solving

- can give effective presentations

- have good communication skills

- can write reports and other kinds of documents

- are enthusiastic and passionate about what you do

- are professional and reliable

- would fit in well with the company / institute – both in terms of the environment and the core values

You need to inject each section of your CV with evidence that you have the above attributes. The following chapters will tell you how.

Here is an extract from an email from an HR manager to a recruiting agency:

IRC: post-doc position   Inbox   x

Adrian Wallwork <adrian.wallwork@gmail.com>
to me

The candidate should have:

- Excellent communication skills

- Analytical thinking - be able to build patterns from raw data
- Be able to write succinct reports in English to tight deadlines
- Be a go getter, self motivator, who can work fairly independently

If you were applying for the post indicated in the email above, your CV would need to demonstrate that you have such qualities.

For example, by writing that you have had 12 research papers accepted at international conferences you are indicating that: 1) you can write technical documents; 2) you have experience in presenting your work; 3) your English is probably of a high standard.

1.3 What are research institutes really looking for? And companies? (cont.)

You should not state directly, either in your CV or cover letter, that 'I have good communication skills' as such skills are subjective and difficult for the recruiter to evaluate. Instead the recruiter should be able to understand that you have these skills from the evidence that you provide of your education, work experience and personal interest sections (see Chapters 6, 7 and 8).

1.4 Is it a good idea to send the same CV to different companies / institutes?

No.

You need to tailor (customize) your CV for the specific post you are applying for.

You could start by drafting a CV that contains everything that anyone could possibly find relevant and interesting. This could require several pages. You then adapt this draft CV to make it read and look as if it was specifically written for that particular company or institute. Adaptation consists of:

- deleting anything that is not strictly relevant. This does not mean removing whole parts from your Education and Work Experience sections, but simply removing elements that are not relevant in any way to that job. This means that you can highlight the key qualifications that you could bring to the post you are applying for.

- modifying the text to make sure that it includes evidence of the skills that you will need for the post you have applied for

- changing the layout and/or font so that it reflects the same graphic style as the company or institute where you want to work

1.5 Do I need to be honest?

Yes.

CVs may be checked for detail using special software. Any discrepancies will be identified immediately. In any case, experienced recruiters can spot a lie very quickly.

Even if the potential employer does not have access to CV-checking software, they will likely cross check your CV with your LinkedIn profile (or profiles on other academic or social media). So ensure that i) what you write is the truth; ii) there is consistency between all your online profiles.

Even just one thing on your CV that is proved wrong during an interview may make the interviewer think that the rest of the CV is not true either. This will immediately undermine any trust that they may have had with you.

If you make claims on your CV which during the interview turn out to be unsubstantiated, you also risk the company informing the recruiting agency, who may then remove you from their database.

1.6 Will recruiters access my Facebook, Instagram and Twitter accounts?

Possibly.

The kind of information – both in the form of text and images – that you post on the Internet is a clear indicator of your personality and of your social behavior and communication style. Also, HR people have a natural human curiosity about potential candidates and will seek out information that is not contained in a CV.

So ensure that you limit who can access your pages. Alternatively, do not post anything online that you would not want to be read or seen by an HR person.

1.7 Should I used LinkedIn?

Yes, although LinkedIn used to seen primarily as a means for getting jobs in industry, it is also becoming increasingly used by academics.

Academics create a LinkedIn profile to:

1. showcase their research
2. boost their chances of finding a job
3. create a network of useful contacts

1.8   Should I consider a video CV?

Video CVs are not common for most types of jobs. The risk is that if you only send a video CV, no one will look at it. Moreover, it is a little more difficult to skim through a video than a written document, thus you are asking for a greater effort on the part of HR.

When a recruiter looks at a CV, he/she can concentrate almost exclusively on the information contained in it. A video CV can be watched from many points of view – not just content, but also the means of presentation (much more so than in a written CV). Your clothes, your voice, your behavior could all distract from what you are saying about yourself and your achievements. Thus the first impression that the recruiter gets may be based on superficialities such as the way you move, your tone, and your smile or lack of it. Such impressions are better left to the face-to-face interview.

However, if video CVs are the norm in your intended work field, then check out other people's video CVs. There are plenty available on YouTube and also on professional recruitment sites.

Watch them and decide what you think works well and what you should avoid.

The ones that often work the best tend to be the simplest. They:

- have no distracters, so that what the HR person sees is much the same as they would see in a good quality Skype call, i.e. you sitting down (preferably in front of a white background) without performing any particular actions
- are shot in one session, i.e. not in a series of different locations at different times

A major issue is your skills in the English language. If you are a non-native speaker:

- ensure that you have your script (i.e. what you say in your video) corrected by a native speaker
- use short sentences (long sentences are more difficult to say)
- only use words that you can pronounce correctly
- enunciate clearly and do no speak too fast

1.9 Is it a good idea to have my CV on my personal website?

Yes. If someone takes the trouble to access your personal website, they will probably also be motivated to read / download your CV.

In this case, you need to write your CV so that it will appeal to as many different types of potential employer as possible within the fields that you are looking for. Or if you are only interested in one specific area, then your online CV should reflect this area.

Chapter 2
Templates and Recruiters

Factoids

❖ One of the first resumes ever written was by Leonardo da Vinci, in which he summarized all his qualifications: *I have kinds of mortars; most convenient and easy to carry; and with these I can fling small stones almost resembling a storm; and with the smoke of these cause great terror to the enemy, to his great detriment and confusion. ... In times of peace I believe I can give perfect satisfaction and to the equal of any other in architecture and the composition of buildings public and private; and in guiding water from one place to another.*

❖ The average boss looks at a CV for three minutes.

❖ Byte London, a marketing technology agency, recently introduced a chatbot (a computer program that conducts a conversation) to help find employees. Replacing the initial application process, the Facebook Messenger chatbot, named Space Gentleman, asks applicants a series of 10 questions such as: "Do you have the right to work in the UK?"

❖ In 2014 Google received more than 20,000 resumes a week, or two every minute. That figure has now doubled - Google gets two million applications per year and is 10 times more difficult to get into than Harvard University.

❖ In 2013, Google returned around 3 million pages in response to the search 'CV templates', today it returns 122 million. Many of these are free downloadable templates from which you can then create your own CV. You can also view sample CVs specifically tailored, for example, for mechanical engineers, teachers, chefs, financial analyst, or those wanting a place in medical school or in marketing.

© Springer Nature Switzerland AG 2019
A. Wallwork, *English for Academic CVs, Resumes, and Online Profiles*,
English for Academic Research, https://doi.org/10.1007/978-3-030-11090-1_2

2.1   What's the buzz?

A) How many pages should a CV have?

- one

- two

- content is more important than the number of pages

B) What sections does a CV typically have? e.g. education, work experience

C) Imagine you are a recruiter whose job is to assess CVs and resumes. Look at the nine factors below - which do you think would be the top three?

- Clear objective

- Computer skills

- Easy to read

- Education

- Individuality/desire to succeed

- Personal experiences

- Qualifications and skills

- Related work experience

- Spelling and grammar

D) Look at the key to this chapter where you will find the results of a survey of recruiters carried out in the USA. Note: the recruiters were not primarily recruiting recent graduates.

Answer these questions:

1. Which for you are the most surprising results of the survey?

2. What do the results highlight in terms of choosing a template for your CV?

3. In your CV, did you use a standard template (which one?) or did you create your own?

4. What are the pros and cons of creating your own template?

5. Which of the following would you not use in your CV? Why?

- colored fonts

- comic sans

- logos of the institutes or companies where you have worked

6. How quickly do you think recruiters read a CV?

2.1 What's the buzz? (cont.)

In this chapter you will learn the ideal number of pages for a CV, the typical order of information in a CV, and how fast recruiters are likely to read your CV. Various templates (layouts and styles) are discussed, including the Europass, as well has how to customize them. LinkedIn is focused on in terms of how it differs from a traditional CV, what potential employers want to see on your LinkedIn page, and how recruiters and HR use LinkedIn to find potential candidates.

2.2 How many pages should a CV be?

Your ability to be concise and to only highlight your most relevant skills and qualifications is revealed through your CV. If your CV is more than two pages, the HR person may think 'this person is unable to express themself clearly and concisely; this is not the kind of person I want working in my company'.

However, if you are looking for certain high-level or high-profile jobs in academia, it may be appropriate to use more pages so that you have space to describe the projects you have been involved in. If you have a lot of publications, put them in a separate document or just have a link to your website where the professor (or whoever is dealing with your application) can download them if he / she wishes.

2.3 What is the typical order of information in a CV?

The most common order is outlined below.

1. name (Chapter 3)
2. personal details (Chapter 3)
3. objective / short profile (Chapter 4)
4. personal statements, biographies (Chapter 5)
5. education (Chapter 6)
6. work experience (Chapter 7)
7. skills (Chapter 8)
8. personal interests (Chapter 9)
9. publications (Chapter 5)
10. references (Chapter 10)

There are of course variations in this order. Some people put point 3 before point 2. If you are an academic you may put your publications (point 8) into a separate document. If you not an academic and have work experience, then you will probably put your work experience before your education. The skills section may be divided into subsections (e.g. technical, languages). Not everyone mentions their personal interests though I would argue that these are essential. Not everyone puts references.

If you are not applying for a job in academia, then your publications will be of little interest to the recruiter.

Not all templates will include all the nine points above.

2.4 What is a template? Should I use one?

A template is a document that shows a layout and sample content. The template puts the information required (i.e. points 1-9 in the previous section) into a specific order.

Downloadable templates can be found in the appendix to this book.

Your aim is to facilitate the work of the recruiter who reads your CV. Consequently, it makes sense to use a template, or at least a format, that a recruiter will be familiar with and with which they can make quick comparisons with CVs of other candidates. If necessary you can modify the format of your CV to make your CV stand out from the hundreds of others that the recruiter will be reading.

The popularity and importance of LinkedIn mean that CVs tend to look more and more like a LinkedIn profile, in terms of both layout and content. So check out the layout that LinkedIn are currently using, and if appropriate, adapt it for your CV.

In some cases your potential employer will provide you with their own template to fill in. If this is the case, follow their instructions carefully. Do not try to adapt their template to fit your wishes. Alternatively, you may be requested to use a particular standard template.

When writing a CV for a specific company or institute, find the CV (e.g. via LinkedIn) of someone who already works there and model your CV on theirs.

2.5 How fast do recruiters read CVs? Do all recruiters read CVs in the same way?

Recruiters typically take around 6 seconds to make an initial evaluation.

The picture below shows two versions of the CV of the same person. patches indicate the amount of heat from a recruiter's eyes on the page when looking two different CVs. The darker the patch, the longer the recruiter spent looking at that particular point in the CV.

A comparison between the two CVs reveals that the recruiter stopped looking at the first CV before reaching the bottom of the page, whereas the second CV received the full attention of the recruiter. But why?

The answer is simple: the first CV has a series of blocks of text. The second CV divides the information up into more manageable portions. Moral of the story: How you lay out your CV will have a huge impact on whether a human reader will read it all or not. If they stop reading, you are unlikely to be shortlisted for the job.

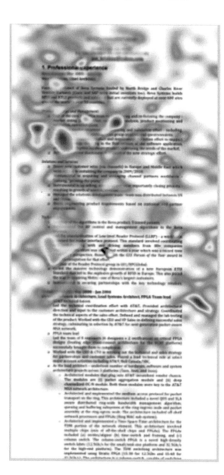 

2.5 How fast do recruiters read CVs? Do all recruiters read CVs in the same way? (cont.)

Bear in mind that although most recruiters will start at the top and work down, some may start at the bottom and work up. This means that wherever the reader chooses to begin reading, what they read must be perfectly clear and make perfect sense.

As with all kinds of writing, you need to imagine that you are the reader, in this case a recruiter. Don't think of ways to impress the recruiter. Instead think: how can I make my CV easy and quick to read? This means:

- understanding and facilitating the priorities of the recruiter (i.e. their top priority is to find the right candidate in the minimum time possible with the minimum effort)
- avoiding big chunks of text
- avoiding unnecessary information (e.g. if you are a PhD student applying for a job in industry, the recruiter will probably not appreciate seeing the long list of papers that you have published)

For more information about the heat map (including a color version) shown in the picture see:

https://www.fastcodesign.com/1669531/how-to-redesign-your-resume-for-a-recruiter-s-6-second-attention-span

2.6 Isn't the information contained in my CV more important to a recruiter than the layout?

No, not initially.

Recruiters' eyes tend to focus on the left hand side of the page. This is probably due to the fact that in standard well laid out CVs, the dates and key words (i.e. job positions, names of companies and universities) tend to be found on the left.

Like all readers, a recruiter's eye is drawn towards white space and initial capital letters. This means that we focus more on the beginnings and ends of sentences, than we do on the middle of sentences. It also means that CVs that have big blocks of dense text tend to be read with less interest than those where the content has been divided up into short blocks of text.

So, your CV may be quickly discarded if:

- key achievements are hidden within a big blocks of texts
- you deviate from the standard presentation, i.e. if your dates and key words do not appear on the left

The way your CV is laid out is thus crucial if you want a recruiter to look at it for more than a couple of seconds.

2.7 How can I help recruiters understand what the most important information is on CV?

Highlight the importance of particular achievements or skills by giving them more space (i.e. more words, more lines of text).

If you give as much space to your work experience in a shop as to your work experience in a professor's laboratory, this gives the impression that the two experiences were of equal importance.

2.8 How does a LinkedIn page differ from a traditional CV?

Your LinkedIn page will differ from your CV in the following areas:

1) Your connections and endorsements: these are things that you cannot build overnight and which may help the recruiter to see:

   • how good your networking skills are

   • who you are connected to (there is a chance the recruiter may have common connections with you)

   • who has endorsed you and for what. However, recruiters are aware that LinkedIn invites members to endorse each other and that such endorsements may be given without much thought

2) People who have recommended you (see Chapter 10 on writing references). If someone has taken the time and trouble to recommend you, this should indicate that they think you made a valuable contribution in some area. But again recruiters are aware that some people write their own recommendations for friends and colleagues to post.

3) Your photo. Although photos are frequently found on CVs (see Chapter 3), they are even more frequently found on LinkedIn as the site encourages you to post your photo.

2.9 What do potential employers want to see on my LinkedIn page?

First they will probably look at high level details in your profile: who you have worked for and when, and what your job title was (and what this involved), i.e. the same things they look for on a CV. From this information they will get a sense of whether each experience has built upon the previous one and whether you are following some specific direction – again similarly to a CV.

2.10   How do recruiters and HR use LinkedIn?

In two ways.

1) Active recruitment. This means they use LinkedIn to find candidates. These are just potential candidates who may not even be on the job market. The recruiter types in keywords (e.g. *Master's in xxx, three years' experience in yyy*) so that they can find people who could potentially recruit. They then email these people and present the company to them. Their aim is to arrange an interview with potential candidates.

2) Recruitment via an advertisement. The company or institute places an ad on LinkedIn and then receives CVs from potential candidates.

2.11   Do recruitment agencies ask candidates to use a particular template?

Recruiters may ask you to frame your CV into a particular template. This does not allow much in terms of customization, but you can still decide the actual words you use in each of the blocks of the template.

Do not compile your CV or answers to any questions directly online.

1. First print off the template.

2. Analyse your existing CV and decide which parts could go into the template.

3. Modify these parts so that they are completely relevant for the position.

4. For those blocks in the template that remain, write your answers offline.

5. Put all the text that you plan to use into one file. Re-read it several times and then do a final spell check.

6. Copy and paste the text into the relevant places.

Decide what key words their software is likely to look for (look for the key words in their adverts, or on their website) and try to integrate them into your CV

Not all recruiters request you to use their own template. Monster (monster.com), which is one of world's biggest employment websites and job search engine, provides a series of downloadable templates:

https://www.monster.co.uk/career-advice/article/monster-cv-template

2.12 I want to be different. Should I create my own layout and style?

Probably not.

To understand why, try this experiment. Find five examples of CVs from friends, family or from Google Images. Ignore any CVs that follow a standard template (e.g. the Europass).

Look at each CV for a maximum of two seconds. Which ones do you like and not like? Why? What impression of the candidate do you get? Think about:

- how pleasing the CV looks
- what order the information is presented
- how easy it would be for recruiters to find the key information they are interested in

Then, imagine you are the HR person, and that these CVs are just five of the 250 that you have received for the same job. What would be your main problem with deciding which candidates to reject and which to interview?

You will probably notice:

- the incredible variety of presentation, layout and formatting styles
- that even the name of the candidate does not appear in the same place in each CV
- that the order of information is not the same (some begin with work experience, others with academic experience, and others with a personal objective)
- the massive difference in the way the candidates present their personal details and the abbreviations they use, not all of which will be familiar to all recruiters
- the different headings for the same kind of activity (e.g. work experience, professional experience, employment history)

What is also interesting is that presumably the people who wrote these CVs were satisfied with what they had produced.

So what is the net result for the recruiter who is faced with a massive variety of formats? Answer: confusion.

The recruiter has to work extra hard to find the information that he / she wants and to be able to compare the same information across several CVs.

2.12 I want to be different. Should I create my own layout and style? (cont.)

If you were the recruiter, would you not prefer to receive the same information in the same way from all the candidates? Then you could focus primarily on comparing the experiences of the candidates rather than wasting time having to actually identify this experience and being distracted by different layouts.

So if you decide to be creative and to produce your own original CV template, you need to be aware that it may be detrimental to your chances of your CV being read and thus of you ever being invited to an interview. This is true in the majority of areas of both industry and research, possible exceptions may be in media and advertising, where having a creative CV may indicate a creative mind.

2.13   What about spacing between lines, paragraphs and sections? And bullets? Fonts?

Compare these two versions - which is easier to read? The font in both cases is Calibri, 10 point.

VERSION 1: NOT SPACED (CRAMPED), MIX OF ALL CAPS AND LOWER CASE, BULLETS

LANGUAGES
- Chinese   mother tongue
- English   fluent (spoken and written)

AWARDS AND HONORS
- Young Scientist award, *POLYCHAR 19 - World Forum on Advanced Materials,* Nepal, 2029.
- Best Poster Award, *Fluoropolymer 2028*, Mèze, France.
- Excellent Graduate of Shanghai, ECUST, China, 2027.

References
- Prof. Giulia Gestri (in whose lab I did more than 4 years of research work), Department of Chemistry and Industrial Chemistry, University of Pisa. gestri@xxx.it

VERSION 2: SPACED (6 PT BETWEEN SECTIONS, 2 PT WITHIN SECTIONS), NO CAPS, NO BULLETS

Languages
Chinese: mother tongue; English: fluent (spoken and written)

Awards and Honors
Young Scientist award, POLYCHAR 19 - World Forum on Advanced Materials, Nepal, 2029.
Best Poster Award, Fluoropolymer 2028, Mèze, France.
Excellent Graduate of Shanghai, ECUST, China, 2027.

References
Prof. Giulia Gestri (in whose lab I did more than 4 years of research work), Department of Chemistry and Industrial Chemistry, University of Pisa. gestri@xxx.it

Version 2 occupies marginally more space, but is cleaner and much easier to read: no bullets, no capitals in headings, no italics. The idea is to make it easy on the readers eye.

Among the clearest fonts to read are Arial, Calibri and Verdana.

Use between 10 pt and 11 pt. Anything smaller is difficult to read and will look as if you have tried to include too much text, rather than finding ways to be more concise.

2.13 What about spacing between lines, paragraphs and sections? And bullets? Fonts? (cont.)

Show your CV in different formats to as many people as possible, then see if you can reach some consensus as to which is easiest to read.

Consider using the same font as is used by the company or institute where you are sending your CV - it gives the impression that you already work there!

2.14 What is the Europass? Why and how should I modify it?

In Europe, one of the most commonly used templates is the Europass Curriculum Vitae, which you can create online at the Europass site: https://europass.cedefop. europa.eu/

The Europass is typically the format required for students to gain positions at universities and research centers in Europe.

Its main advantages are:

- the Europass template is easy for you to compile and the instructions on the site are easy to follow

- it has a familiar format for most academic employers in Europe. This means that a secretary or professor, for example at a university department, knows exactly where to find particular information about you within your CV.

- it is easy for a potential employer to quickly compare your qualifications and experience with those of other candidates that have used the Europass template.

The main disadvantages are that it:

- typically produces a CV of more than three pages due to its wasteful use of the left-hand column (see first example below)

- has some sections that are probably best avoided e.g. 'communication skills'

- does not have a section for a profile / summary section at the top of the CV

Below are two versions of identical information. Note how the second version requires considerably less space.

Education and training	
Dates	2028-2031
Title of qualification awarded	PhD
Principal subjects/occupational skills covered	Thesis Title: 'Young People in the Construction of the Virtual University', empirical research that directly contributes to debates on e-learning.
Name and type of organisation providing education and training	Brunel University, London, UK Funded by an Economic and Social Research Council Award

2.14 What is the Europass? Why and how should I modify it? (cont.)

	Education and training
2028-2031	PhD (ISCED 6), funded by an Economic and Social Research Council Award at Brunel University, London, UK
	Thesis Title: 'Young People in the Construction of the Virtual University', empirical research that directly contributes to debates on e-learning.

The modifications made in the second version should help you to reduce a 3-4 page CV based on a standard template into a 2-page CV.

2.15 I have decided to use a template. What can I customize?

If you have decided yourself to use a particular template, and the institute where you are going to send your CV has made no specific requests regarding the format, then you can customize as you wish. However the final result must match the standard norms, e.g. the usual order that information is presented.

Of course, there may be more than one 'usual' order. But some sections tend always to appear in the same place. This means that you should not put your personal information at the end of the CV, given that most recruiters will expect to find it at the beginning.

Recruiters can learn a lot about you from the layout of your CV (e.g. how well organized you are, whether you are a good communicator), so be careful how you deviate from the standard.

Customizing can be made in many areas.

CHANGE THE SECTION TITLES

Instead, for example, using the term 'Personal information' you could write 'Personal Details' (note the use of initial capital letters for both words).

CHANGE THE ORDER OF THE SECTIONS

Many templates with 'Personal information' and is followed by 'Desired employment / Occupational field'. Many candidates reverse the order of these two sections to give prominence to the type of job they are applying for.

CHANGE THE ORDER OF INFORMATION WITHIN A SECTION

In the Work experience section in some templates, the name and address of the employer is the fourth item, you might wish to put this information in first position, particularly if you have studied at a prestigious university or done an internship in an internationally well-known company

CHANGE THE FONT

The Europass uses Arial Narrow which is a nice clear readable font that does not occupy too much space. However, some people find it a little too small to read. Alternatives could be Arial (normal), Helvetica, Verdana, and Calibri - all of which are easy to read and fairly standard. Avoid using strange fonts (they may get you noticed but for the wrong reasons) and never use Comic Sans (or similar fonts) as it is often associated with children.

2.15 I have decided to use a template. What can I customize? (cont.)

CHANGE THE COLOR

Some templates are just in black and white. You could use grey or blue for headers. In any case stick to one font and two colors. Use bold but avoid italics (unless in titles of books, papers or theses). The idea is that your CV should look clear, the more fonts, colors and formatting types you use, the more difficult it will be to read.

ADD A NEW SECTION

You can add sections that don't appear in the standard template (e.g. personal interests, references).

2.16   Templates and Recruiters: Do's and Don'ts

➢ Do spend a lot of time preparing your CV - it is one of the most important documents you will ever write.

➢ Do research your chosen organization and find out what they expect to see in a CV. Tailor your CV specifically to your chosen organization - try to keep all the info relevant, if it won't help you get the job then consider deleting it.

➢ Do <u>not</u> follow your own personal opinions of how a CV should be written and laid out, stick to what will be familiar for the reader.

➢ Do <u>not</u> write from your own point of view. Instead, write from the hirer's / employer's point of view.

➢ Do use a clear layout. If it doesn't attract attention within 2-3 seconds, it will not be read in full.

➢ Be concise - keep your CV to a max of 2 pages (excluding Publications). Your CV is not your life story.

➢ Do <u>not</u> use a template that has been written in your own language (use the English version of Europass, not for instance, the French, Spanish or Italian one). The risk is that you may inadvertently leave parts of the CV (e.g. headings, footers) in your own language

➢ Do modify your chosen template to keep it to two pages, and to make it as concise, clean and readable as possible.

➢ Do <u>not</u> modify a template that has been specifically provided by your chosen organization.

Whatever you decide:

• use a readable font (e.g. Arial, Calibri)

• no smaller than 10 pt

• clear spacing between sections - lots of white space

• limit the use of bold and capitals and in any case always use them for the same function

• only use color if you are convinced it will increase your chances of getting a job

• ensure that you haven't left any text in your own language

Chapter 3
Personal Information

Factoids

❖ Surnames in Thailand only came into existence in 1913, when every family was asked to choose their own last name.

❖ In Iceland, boys' and girls' surnames consist of the father's first name + son / daughter, e.g. the footballer Aron Gunnarsson (= Gunnar's son) and the singer Björk Guðmundsdóttir (= Guðmund's daughter). This means that members of the same family may all have different surnames.

❖ In experiments males have been given pictures of equally attractive females, but with more or less attractive names (Kathy, Jennifer, Christine as opposed to Ethel, Harriet and Gertrude). Those with attractive names were judged to be more physically attractive.

❖ In some parts of the world, people do not have a family name. For example, the Ethiopian name Yohannes Gedamu Gebre is in the order of given name, father's given name and grandfather's given name. However, given that the reader of your CV is unlikely to have this knowledge, the solution is to treat the third name as the surname when applying for a job.

❖ Some Chinese people give themselves an English nickname in order to facilitate communication with people outside China. However, on your CV you should write your official Chinese name (though obviously using Latin characters and not Chinese ones). If you use your English nickname, the recruiter might think that the English name is your real name and thus that may be your mother or father are from an Anglo country.

© Springer Nature Switzerland AG 2019
A. Wallwork, *English for Academic CVs, Resumes, and Online Profiles*,
English for Academic Research, https://doi.org/10.1007/978-3-030-11090-1_3

3.1 What's the buzz?

A) Which of the following do you think you should be obliged by law to put on your CV? Why (not)? To learn more about the legislation regarding CVs see the key at the end of this chapter.

❑ your full name

❑ date of birth

❑ gender

❑ race

❑ marital status

❑ email address

❑ mobile phone number

B) Which of the following do you think it is also a good idea to include? Why (not)?

❑ whether you have children

❑ your postal address

❑ links to personal website

❑ link to your LinkedIn profile

❑ links to your ResearchGate, Academia, etc profiles

❑ your home phone number

❑ an explanation (how?) of whether you name is male or female (if this is not clear from the name itself and you don't put a photo). Note that names such as Michel, Andrea, Emanuele can be male or female depending on the country.

❑ Skype (or similar) number

❑ your fax number

❑ your personal website

❑ Facebook, Instagram, Twitter, etc accounts

❑ whether you have completed your military service

❑ the fact that you have a driving license

C) Discuss the pros and cons of NOT including a photograph of yourself. If you opt for a photo, how do you choose the photo?

3.1 What's the buzz? (cont.)

This chapter tells you how and where you should write your name, whether you should include a photo and if so what type, and how you should I write your date of birth. You will learn the importance of having a professional-looking email address, and how to present yourself on LinkedIn.

3.2   How should I write my name?

In Anglo countries such as the USA and the UK, people write their names as follows:

1. given name (i.e. the name your parents gave you), also known as 'first name'

2. family name (i.e. the last name of your father / mother), also known as 'surname' or 'last name'

For example, James Bond and not Bond James.

If in your country you do not follow the same standard, then it is your decision whether you conform to the Anglo system on your English CV.

Imagine you are from, for instance, Vietnam, and your name is Bui Thanh Liem: Bui is the family name, Thanh the middle name, and Liem the given name. I suggest you put Bui Thanh Liem at the top of your CV, i.e. following the same order as in your country. This is order that most people will search for you on the internet.

However, at the interview you could explain that your given name is Liem.

3.3   Where should I write my name?

Irrespectively of the type of template you use, the first words at the top of your CV should be your name. This will enable the recruiter to find your CV quickly.

I suggest you:

- write your name as outlined in 3.2

- use a bigger font size than the rest of the CV

- use bold

- center your name or at least put it in a prominent position

Below are two examples. The second examples reduces the unnecessary space occupied by the first example.

EXAMPLE 1 (8 LINES)

Personal information	
Surname(s) / First name(s)	**Caturgli Elisa**
Address(es)	Via Carducci 9, 56126 Pisa (Italy)
Telephone(s)	0039 050 314 5750
E-mail	elisa.caturgli@gmail.com
Nationality	Italian
Date of birth	27/01/1997
Gender	female

EXAMPLE 2 (5 LINES)

Elisa Caturgli

Biotechnologist

elisa.caturgli@gmail.com
0039 340 7888 3147
27/01/1986
Italian

3.3 Where should I write my name? (cont.)

Note Example 2:

- does not contain the term *curriculum vitae* or *resume* (there can be no doubt to the reader what this document is). Instead it contains the candidate's name

- does not contain any heading. It is obvious that these are personal / contact details, so there is no need for a heading saying 'Personal Information'

- puts the given name before the family name (this is the most common order in the Anglo world)

- the personal details are minimal and occupy little space

- the qualification / role of the candidate (biotechnologist) is immediately clear

EXAMPLE 3 (3 LINES)

An alternative, if you decide not to put your photo:

Elisa Caturgli

Biotechnologist

27/01/1986, Italian, elisa.caturgli@gmail.com, 0039 050 314 5750

3.4 Should I include a photograph?

You may decide not to put a photo in solidarity with those people who be discriminated against on the basis of their race / color and / or name. In reality there is no real reason why an employer or professor in a research group should need to know what you look like. Looks should be irrelevant to the world of research and academia, only brains and talent should count.

However, if the hirer expects a photograph then it makes sense to include one. Even if you don't like the idea of putting your photo on your CV you should try to satisfy the recruiter's requirements, not your own personal preferences. So if requested, include a photo.

If the hirer specifically asks you not to include a photograph then do not include one. For example, there may be Equal Opportunities legislation which prohibits them from hiring on the basis of gender or other types of discrimination.

Otherwise there are no clear guidelines to follow.

Some HR people find the photo distracting, particularly when they are totally indifferent about whether to employ a woman or a man.

However, small companies or research groups may be curious to know what you look like and how old you are. This is because you may potentially be a future colleague (or boss) of the person who reads your CV or interviews you. In such cases, if you do not include a photograph, they may try to find one on Facebook or other social / work network.

So if you think there is a chance that your hirer may want to see what you look like, then either include a photograph, or at least make sure there is nothing compromising on your Facebook page!

3.5   I have decided to include my photo. What kind of photo should I choose?

Your photo is your image. It could potentially tell the recruiter a lot about you:

- your personality - are you smiling? is it a sincere smile?
- your attitude to your appearance - the clothes you are wearing
- your level of professionalism - how much trouble you have taken to choose an appropriate photo, e.g. not a photo that was clearly never intended to be put on a CV

In order not to distract the recruiter, your photo should be as 'neutral' as possible. This means:

- a professional passport type photo that has been taken recently
- passport size
- centered
- no background
- black and white

A black and white photo tends to look more professional and also photocopies / prints better than a color photo.

Whatever photo you choose it should be positioned on the left or right of the page, not right in the center. It should not be the main feature of attention.

3.6   What are the qualities of a good photograph?

Look at the photos of your connections on LinkedIn and decide which ones you think would be the most appropriate for a CV. What you will probably notice is that the photos you have chosen have the following in common:

- the background is white and empty
- the candidate is in the exact center of the photo, there is not too much space above the head or below the shoulders
- he / she looks professional (smart clothes, neat hair style)
- he / she has a friendly expression (probably smiling)
- the photo would look good even if photocopied in black and white

3.7 How should I write my date of birth?

The simplest way to write a date in a CV is the day as a number, the month as a word, and the year.

> 11 October 2030

Visually, this is the least confusing layout for dates.

Another standard way, often used in the USA, is:

> October 11, 2030

The first system is clearer because the two numbers are separate and there is no need for a comma. You can use the same system when writing the date in a letter (e.g. in your cover letter).

3.8 How 'professional' does my email address need to look?

Your email address reflects your level of professionalism. Avoid any of the following types of address:

> lordofdarkness@yahoo.com (name of favorite rock band, movie etc)

> andrew1999@hotmail.com (first name + number / date of birth)

> verwhite@gmail.com (merge of first name and second name, i.e. Veronica White)

Instead, clearly differentiate your first name from your last name. Here is my address:

> adrian.wallwork@gmail.com

It looks professional and no one is going to get a negative impression from it. Also it will be easy for someone to find your address within their email system.

Clearly, finding a gmail address with your given name + family name is almost impossible today, unless you have an unusual name. So one solution is to add a descriptive word (in my case 'author'), e.g.

> adrian.wallwork.author@gmail.com

3.9   How should I present myself on LinkedIn?

NAME: Do not use any titles e.g. *Dr, Professor*, or any qualifications e.g. *MSc, PhD*. Instead simply write your given name and family name.

PHOTO: See 3.6 to learn how to choose the most appropriate photo.

CONTACT INFO: Some people will message you directly on LinkedIn, but some may prefer to email you. So provide an email address, which does not have to be your regular address but could also be one you set up specifically to deal with LinkedIn enquiries.

3.10   On LinkedIn, what should I put under 'Advice for contacting'?

You can write anything you want here. Typically you can tell people:

- what you would like to be contacted about (e.g. jobs, projects)
- how you want people to contact you (e.g. your email address)

My section is as follows:

adrian.wallwork@gmail.com

I am interested in writing textbooks in the fields of scientific and business English.

My company is also specialized in revising, editing and proofreading scientific manuscripts written by non-native English researchers.

I also offer courses in how to write and present scientific work.

So I have given my email address and advertised my three skills / services: book writing, editing and English courses.

3.11   Personal information: Do's and Don'ts

➤ Do spend a lot of time preparing your CV - it is one of the most important documents you will ever write.

➤ Use only one phone number and preferably a mobile number, then you will always be contactable. Also, you avoid the recruiter having to make a decision about which number to call.

➤ Include one email address, preferably your personal email address (rather than a work address) or possibly your university email address (if you are in research).

➤ In the West, the order of your name is given name + family name.

➤ If your name contains a lot of accents and diacretics and is not a name known in Europe or the US, then it is probably simpler not to put the accents and diacretics. For example, a name such as Trần Ánh Nguyệt is probably better written as Tran Anh Nguyet.

➤ When you need to write the full date, do <u>not</u> use any other system than the two indicated in 3.7. <u>So</u> do not use these:

October 11th, 2020 (you might write 11st or 11rd by mistake)

10.11.20 (in the US this means November 10, in most of the rest of the world it means October 11)

➤ Do choose a photo that is reflects how you really look (rather than your ideal image of yourself!). Never use a selfie!

➤ You are not normally obliged to put a photo. However, a good simple black and white photo is unlikely to detract from your CV and may satisfy the curiosity of the hirer.

➤ Head shot only, centered on a white background. Make sure your hair and any visible clothes look professional. If possible, have a natural smile. In any case try to look friendly.

Chapter 4
Objectives and Personal Profiles

Factoids

❖ According to a survey conducted by ORCID (the Open Researcher and Contributors ID repository) only 50% of researchers have an online profile.

❖ Experts recommend that a personal profile should be between 50 and 200 words.

❖ LinkedIn was launched in 2003. It has been described as the 'de facto tool for professional networking' and has over half a billion users in more than 200 countries. It is in the top 40 most popular websites on the internet.

❖ Academia.edu is a social networking website for academics who wish to share papers and monitor how many people are reading them. It has over 20 million uploaded texts.

❖ A 2016 article in Times Higher Education reported that in a global survey of 20,670 people who use academic social networking sites, ResearchGate was the dominant network and was twice as popular as others: 61 percent of respondents who had published at least one paper had a ResearchGate profile.

❖ Mendeley is a desktop and web program produced by Elsevier for managing and sharing research papers.

❖ Given that one study found that recruiters spend 8.8 seconds looking at a CV. If a candidate has a personal profile this enables recruiters to do their job quickly and decide whether to read the CV or not.

© Springer Nature Switzerland AG 2019
A. Wallwork, *English for Academic CVs, Resumes, and Online Profiles*,
English for Academic Research, https://doi.org/10.1007/978-3-030-11090-1_4

4.1 What's the buzz?

(A) When you write a personal profile, your aim is to tell your potential future employee about your accomplishments.

    1. Can you define 'accomplishment'?

    2. Can you think of some types of typical accomplishment?

    3. What is the difference between an accomplishment and a duty?

(B) For each of the seven activities below, find at least two matching verbs from the box.

    1. assessing   _____   _____   _____

    2. completing   _____   _____   _____

    3. demonstrating   _____   _____   _____

    4. managing   _____   _____   _____

    5. identifying   _____   _____   _____

    6. improving   _____   _____   _____

    7. writing   _____   _____   _____

---

achieve, analyse, assemble, calculate, contribute, control, coordinate, create, design, determine, develop, devise, diagnose, discover, draw, edit, evaluate, examine, expand, formulate, generate, highlight, implement, improve, initiate, install, monitor, observe, oversee, plan, prevent, propose, prove, provide, report, reveal, review, revise, select, set up, solve, test, train, translate, upgrade

---

Now select 5-10 of the verbs that you think you could usefully insert in a profile of yourself to describe your duties, but above all your accomplishments.

(C) Think about your last 4-5 years. For each academic year, list three things that have you accomplished both academically and outside university. Which of these accomplishments would be worth mentioning in your personal profile?

(D) Can you spot the ambiguity in these sentences taken from an applicant's Objective (see 4.2)? Rewrite the sentences so that they would be immediately clear to an HR person.

    (1) A position as a technical surveyor of seismic threats in a private company.

    (2) A position offering opportunities to demonstrate expertise and progress in the field of drafting specifications for software.

4.1 What's the buzz? (cont.)

> (3) A private industry challenging training position focusing on alternative career work style development

In this chapter you will discover the pros and cons of using an Objective in your CV (i.e. a one-line statement of the type of job you are looking for). The chapter details how to write and structure a personal profile / career summary, along with the style and tenses you should use. You will learn how to make your statements sound more dynamic, how to use key words, and how to your profile to the job specifications. Additional tips for writing a profile on LinkedIn, Academia and Research Gate are also given.

4.2 What is an Objective?

A typical resume contains a short summary at the top of the resume (i.e. the first section after the candidate's name). An Objective states what kind of job you would like. Typically it is used when you are not responding to a specific advert. Instead you are sending your CV in the hope that the recruiter or HR person may have a suitable job for you.

In a CV the Objective is located immediately under your personal details.

Maria Alvarez

maria.alvarez@virgilio.it, +68 340 7888 3455

Objective: Position in translational medicine lab as a technician.

Note how the Objective does not require a section heading, but the word *Objective* should simply be inserted before the statement itself.

The Objective should contain as many key words as possible. In the example below, the candidate's Objective is too generic. There are no key words that a search engine would be able to find.

General management position utilizing extensive expertise in a major organization.

It would be better to write:

Junior management position in a Fortune 500 company utilizing 3 years' expertise in financial IT.

An Objective is NOT essential - see 4.4.

4.3 What should I write in my Objective?

Below are some examples.

A researcher in animal psychology seeking a permanent position in a university veterinary hospital.

A PhD student in Business Studies looking for a six-month internship in a commercial bank.

A position in a private industry as a technical surveyor of seismic threats.

A position requiring expertise as a risk analyst in an company exporting to the Far East

Ensure that you do not talk about the benefits for <u>you</u> of working for them. Below is an example of what <u>not</u> to write.

NO! *I am interested in a position where I can further my knowledge of x and gain experience in y.*

In the sentence above, the candidate implies that he is only interested in joining the lab / company so that he can improve himself and further his career. Instead, you should clearly highlight what you can offer the company, i.e. that you have some specific expertise and knowledge and that you are offering this knowledge to the lab / company for their benefit rather than solely yours:

A position that enables me to exploit my background in x and offer my experience of z.

In both examples above the candidate's final aim is the same (to gain experience) but the way he expresses it is totally different: in the first the focus is on him, in the second the focus is more on the hirer.

Below are some more good examples:

A career in engineering physics with a special focus on materials science and engineering.

Employment in the foodservice industry, particularly the healthcare sector.

A position in teaching, specializing in helping children with learning disorders.

A profession in veterinary medicine with emphasis on agriculture and animal production.

4.4 Is writing an Objective always a good idea?

No, not always.

There are two main disadvantages of having an Objective:

1. essentially you are telling the employer what you want, rather than how you might meet their needs

2. you are limiting yourself to what you think you want, but maybe the same company has similar jobs on offer but will not consider you as the similar job doesn't match what you have written on your objective

So rather than an Objective is might be best to begin your CV / resume with a career summary or profile where you highlight to the potential employer how you can add value to their institute, lab, company etc.

4.5 What is a personal profile / career summary? Where in my CV / resume should it be located?

A personal profile / career summary briefly details your career highlights and is often used when you are applying for a specific advertised job. It is a summary of who you are and enables the recruiter to get an instant idea of your qualifications and skills without needing to read the whole CV.

The secret is to highlight your unique skills and achievements, i.e. factors that will differentiate you from other candidates.

Like an Objective, you should place it immediately below your personal details. You do not need a heading, but you might like to make it stand out by using a slightly bigger font, giving it a light grey background, or putting it in a box.

4.6 How should I structure my personal profile and what should it include?

Your profile should be structured so that it answers the following questions:

1) *Who am I? + What kind of job am I looking for?*

The aim is to give the recruiter a one-sentence summary explaining your background and the kind of position you want.

> A recent graduate with an honors degree and Master's in Translational Medicine looking for a position in the research lab of a pharmaceutical company

2) *What can I offer the research team or company?*

Your aim is to sell yourself to the institute or company as the best possible contender for a particular job. See 00 if you are replying to a specific job advert. You need to reveal your relevant skills and support them with evidence.

> During my degree, I developed my communication skills by presenting my research at two national conferences, teaching an undergraduate class, and volunteering at a local hospital.

Note the lack of adjectives that add no tangible value to what you are saying, e.g. *extremely, extensive, excellent, driven, motivated, strategic.*

4.7 What is the best format - one single paragraph or a series of bullet points?

Below are four examples from academia. From a purely visual point of view, which format do you think is:

- easier to read?

- more dynamic?

- would be easier to highlight that your qualifications match the requirements of the institute or industry where you are applying for a job?

FORMAT 1 (ONE PARAGRAPH)

> Five years' experience in molecular biology/genetic engineering of microalgae, focusing on fermentative metabolism and biofuels (hydrogen) in Chlamydomonas reinhardtii. Seven years' experience in plant adaptations to low oxygen levels; highly skilled in rice in vitro culture and transformation, gene cloning, over-expression / silencing, gene expression analyses and proteomics. Able to independently set up protocols and address related problem-solving tasks. Excellent communicative, social and presentation skills combined with strong international background. Currently in the last year of an Alexander von Humboldt postdoctoral fellowship.

Pros: takes up less space than the other formats.

Cons: not as easy to read as the two formats, difficult to pick out key information.

Conclusion: only use if short of space.

FORMAT 2 (HEADINGS RELATED TO EXPERIENCE, EXPERTISE AND INTERESTS)

> **Experience** in syntheses of organic molecules and polymers especially fluorine-containing (meth)acrylate monomers, macromolecular initiators and macromolecules with controlled architecture.
>
> **Good knowledge** of controlled/"living" radical polymerization methods e.g. ATRP, RAFT.
>
> **Future interests**: Supramolecular polymers, well-architectured macromolecules by controlled polymerization, hybrid organic-inorganic nanocomposites ...

Pros: easy to see key information. Allows candidate to mention what he/she would like to do in the future, which is useful if you are not responding to a specific advertisement, but are simply sending your CV to a company or institute in the hope that they might have a position open in your field.

Conclusion: perfect for academic positions.

4.7 What is the best format - one single paragraph or a series of bullet points? (cont.)

FORMAT 3 (BULLET POINTS)

- Over 8 years of experience of **managing an Intellectual Property** department in a large research center with more than 700 research scientists, and building a portfolio of over 200 patent applications in more than 20 countries.
- First-hand experience of licensing negotiations and **successful technology commercialization.**
- Educational background in **Engineering, Management** and **Intellectual Property Rights.**
- **Consultation** to several universities re establishing technology transfer offices.
- More than **70 publications**, including 3 books as author or co-author, 9 peer-reviewed publications, 25 journal and newspaper articles; plus 30 conference papers.
- Teaching at more than **120 workshops on Innovation and IP Management** at universities, research centers, public and private companies.
- Creation of a **website on IP and Innovation Management.**

Pros: easy to see key information, allows candidate to show how he/she matches the requirements in the job description (the order of the bullets could follow the same order as the list of requirements in the advertisement)

Cons: takes up more space than the other formats.

Conclusion: fine if you have sufficient space.

FORMAT 4 (HEADINGS RELATED TO SOFT SKILLS)

A creative and conscientious teacher of English as a foreign language. A recent Trinity Cert. (TESOL) graduate with extensive previous experience in business.

A dynamic, confident verbal and written communicator - in business and in the class room

Innovative and resourceful - an instinctive problem-solver with a flexible approach

Student/stakeholder-focused - enthusiastic and adaptable, committed to achieving results

Organised and reliable - with strong analytical and planning skills

4.7 What is the best format - one single paragraph or a series of bullet points? (cont.)

Pros: easy to see key information. Allows candidate to highlight her soft skills (which are incredibly important in a teaching/learning environment).

Cons: they are such generic skills (any teacher would have them) that they cannot be classified amongst the key words that might be picked up by the software that hirer's use to scan CVs.

Conclusion: suitable for recent graduates with little or no work experience

4.8   What tenses should I use in my personal profile?

The profiles in 4.7 highlight that in most cases you don't need verbs, so the problem of tenses does not arise. However, below is an example where the candidate has begun each bullet with a verb and has correctly used the past simple to refer to past experiences (first three bullets) and the present simple to refer to skills (last bullet).

- Designed over 50 websites for 30 clients in local government
- Optimized internal search engines of existing websites for 10 clients
- Implemented basic monthly maintenance of nearly 100 websites
- Able to use all current web 4.0 technologies

4.9   How can I make my statements sound more dynamic?

Your aim is to provide as much detail as you can thereby enabling recruiters to single you out from the thousands of other applicants. So instead of saying the statements in italics below, you should reformulate them into the second statements.

Responsible for teaching IT skills to undergraduates.

= Created a new curriculum for teaching undergraduates IT skills need to store their research, improve networking, and develop open source software.

Supervised research team in an EU project.

= Led a 4-person research team in a 3-month EU project on food waste.

4.10   How can I match my profile to the job specifications?

Let's imagine the specifications for the job (hereafter job spec) you are applying for are:

WEBSITE DESIGNER

Must be 100% familiar with web 4.0.

At least three years' direct experience.

Excellent knowledge of search engine development.

Should be prepared to carry out also routine work e.g. website maintenance

Fluent English (both spoken and written)

The profile could be written so that it exactly matches the job spec:

- Able to use all current **web 4.0** technologies
- **Four years** experience in **website design**: over 50 websites for 30 clients in local government
- Optimized internal **search engines** of existing websites for 10 clients
- Implemented **basic monthly maintenance** of nearly 100 websites
- **Fluent English** (Cambridge Proficiency, Grade A)

Note how the order of the points in the profile is now the same as the order in the job spec. A recruiter's software will spot all the key words from the job spec that are in the candidate's profile. Also, a human reader will see the key words clearly as they are highlighted in bold and will be able to easily tick off all the items in the job spec.

Note also how the candidate has added her English skills, as these are required in the job spec. Again, this will increase her chances of having her CV shortlisted.

4.10   How can I match my profile to the job specifications? (cont.)

In summary:

- adapt your existing executive summary to match precisely the requirements of the job spec

- put the items in your executive summary in the same order as they appear in the job spec

- add any items that are in the job spec but which were not in your original executive summary

- ensure that you insert all the key words from the job spec and highlight them in bold

4.11 How useful will my profile be for recruiters?

A profile / summary forces you to think about what you kind of position you really want and what skills you possess to obtain such a position.

It is also useful for

1. a hiring manager to immediately see who you are, what you want, and how you might fit in with their hiring plans

2. a recruiting agency to paste into an email to a company who the agency thinks might be interested in you

Below is an email from Simon, a recruiter, who thinks that Carmen, who is a hiring manager in a company, might be interested in a candidate called Juri Nizik.

Position # 1234/65 Juri Nizik

Dear Carmen,

I think you might be interested in Juri Nizik, a very strong candidate:
Nine years of development experience. Strong core Java/J2SE- especially in high performance multi-threaded server development. Excellent knowledge of FIX and messaging based connectivity applications. Currently in last year of PhD in Virtual Robotics at the University of Krakow. Three years of work experience at Lorien Engineering Polska.

Regards,
Simon
ABC Recruitment Ltd

All Simon has done is to paste Juri's executive summary (the part in italics) into the email. This saves Simon a lot of time.

So by including a profile or summary in your CV, you may increase your chances of a recruiting agency sending your curriculum to a firm.

4.12 What key words should I insert in my profiles and how can I insert them?

In theory, the higher the word count, the more instances of a key word a search engine will find.

Key words tend to be of two types: a) technical, b) skills.

Type A key words are typically nouns or adjectives or combinations of the two (*genetics, genetic engineering; Java, Java script; cryptography, cryptographic programming*).

Type B key words are often particular skills that a company requires. Such skills are typically written using the *-ing* form of verbs (e.g. *presenting, managing, problem solving*) and adjectives + nouns (software analysis, performance reviews).

Let's imagine you are trying to encourage recruiters and hirers to contact you for a job.

1. On company or institute websites, find 5-10 descriptions of the type of jobs you would be interested in.

2. Underline the key words in each job description. Remember to include both types A and B.

3. Compile a list of the most frequently used 10 keys words.

4. Think of one or two synonyms for each of these words and add these to the list

5. Choose the top 3-5 key words in your list and insert them into your heading.

6. Use as many key words in as many other places in your profile as possible (with the exception of the Personal Interests and Causes sections). Try to insert them in a natural way, so that a human reader will not feel they are being bombarded by key words - remember that you are writing both for search engines and humans.

If your key words can be expressed by several difference words, you cannot be sure which of these words a potential employer might use, so you should try to insert all of them. For example, I revise the English of manuscripts for publication in scientific journals. This revision process can be described using several different words - *revising, editing, proofreading, correcting*. So I need to insert all of these in my profile. But I also need to insert different forms of the same key word: *revise, revision, revising*. Then I need to consider the kind of documents I am revising, so I need to include: *paper, manuscript, research, thesis* etc.

4.12 What key words should I insert in my profiles and how can I insert them? (cont.)

I am also a teacher of English. My field exploits many acronyms e.g. EFL, ESL, ESOL, CPE, FCE, BESIG. So it makes sense for me to include both the acronym (BESIG) and the full version (business English special interest group).

Using synonyms and different forms of the same words also makes your profile sound more natural.

Obviously in some cases, only very specific key words will be required, which may have no synonyms. But again, if these words have different grammatical forms (infinitive, gerund, noun, adjective, adverb) you can still create some variety.

4.13 How do I write a profile on LinkedIn, Academia and Research Gate?

The content of your profile is likely to be very similar to your CV, but don't simply cut and paste sections from your CV. A LinkedIn profile can be considerably longer than a CV, you can afford to use a less telegraphic and more dynamic style. Your aim throughout your profile is to:

- catch the attention of search engines by using appropriate key words

- showcase your achievements and make yourself sound unique, i.e. different from other people searching for the same kind of job

- highlight your credibility

As on a CV, don't fill your profile with:

- adjectives that could be interpreted as being an exaggeration (e.g. *above average, amazing, cutting edge, highly*)

- expressions that are typically found in millions of profiles (e.g. *proven track record, results oriented, team player, hard worker, good communication skills*).

Your aim is to be factual and accurate. No search engine will be programmed to look for such adjectives and expressions. Moreover they add no value for the recruiter, in fact they detract the reader's attention from the important elements in your profile.

Unlike a CV or bio where some people only use the third person, nearly everyone uses the first person on LinkedIn and on academic networking site.

If you want to write a profile for LinkedIn or any other service:

1. Search for someone you know who has the type of position you are looking for, e.g. if you are a PhD student now, then look for someone who did the same PhD as you in the same institute but from a previous year.

2. Look at their profile - note the length, structure, use of key words, number of paragraphs etc.

3. Compare this profile with two or three other people in the same field who are preferably native speakers - note down any differences.

4. Compile a list of the best features from your analysis at points 2 and 3.

5. Use those features to produce your own profile. Don't post it immediately. Show it to your professor and colleagues. Alter it on the basis of their feedback and do a spelling check.

6. Send the profile to a native English speaker to correct. Given that this profile is the first thing that a potential employer may look at, it needs to be perfect.

7. When you are happy with the profile and you have had it checked by a native speaker and done a final spelling check yourself, then post it.

4.14 Where should I place my profile online?

To see details of sites that host academic profiles, see:

http://guides.library.ubc.ca/academic_profile/Academic_Profilers

https://www.ntnu.no/blogger/ub-teknologi/en/2017/04/25/create-your-researcher-profile-and-make-your-research-more-visible/

https://kentonville.com/profile-workshop/ http://www.scwist.ca/building-an-online-profile-to-benefit-your-academic-career/

https://www-library.ch.cam.ac.uk/create-online-profiles

where you will find a summaries of what each of the following services offers - Academia.edu, ResearchGate, Mendeley, and Google Scholar Citations.

You can also find sample downloads that show how researchers have written their profiles. I suggest you choose researchers in your own field, possibly those who attended the same courses as you (in previous years). You can then model your won profile on theirs. This applies both to specifically academic services such as Academia.edu as well as more business-oriented ones such as LinkedIn.

4.15   Objectives and Profiles: Do's and Don'ts

Objective

➢ One sentence summarizing what kind of job you are looking for (so generally not for a position that has been advertised).

➢ Ensure that it is not ambiguous and docs not focus exclusively on the benefits for you.

Profile

➢ Get straight to the point and be concise.

➢ Provide brief evidence of your skills and experience - the idea is to immediately catch the attention of the recruiter.

➢ Try to create enough space to use a series of bull et   points   each   of   which matches the order of the job spec.

➢ If you are not responding to a specific advertisement, save space by using a single paragraph.

➢ Do not mix the grammatical person – remember either first person (*I*) or third (*he/she*), not both.

In both cases:

➢ Insert key words (i.e. those from advertised job spec, or from job specs in your field).

➢ Tailor it to your chosen organization.

➢ Read it aloud to make sure it flows properly.

➢ Get a native speaker to check it.

Chapter 5
Personal Statements, Bios, and Publications

Extracts from personal statements (all genuine) written by university applicants in the UK.

1. What is physics? I don't know; that's why I want to take it at university.

2. I've been intersted in literature since my mother read Shakespear to me in the womb.

3. Thanks for considering my application and I hope I will here from you soon.

4. I am hoping to pass my driving test so I can drive to -insert uni name here- everyday!

5. Economics is a diverse subject, as economics can be related to anything, especially during economic crisis, which forces to think economically, whereas maths has been long one of my favourite subjects, as mathematics can be applied everywhere, moreover, mathematics is useful in everyday life.

6. I have a black belt in karate and enjoy marital arts.

7. I really want to be a doctor. Please give me a place. My friends think I'll be good.

8. On the 20th of April a great figure in history was born ... It was me, who will go on to make great changes in history as we know it.

9. I am a dynamic figure, often seen scaling walls and crushing ice. I have been known to remodel train stations on my lunch breaks, making them more efficient in the areas of heat retention. I write award-winning operas, I manage time efficiently.

10. I am very good with people because I myself am a person.

11. If I could liken myself to anyone in history it would be Martin Luther King.

12. When I was younger I wanted to be a unicorn.

© Springer Nature Switzerland AG 2019
A. Wallwork, *English for Academic CVs, Resumes, and Online Profiles*,
English for Academic Research, https://doi.org/10.1007/978-3-030-11090-1_5

5.1 What's the buzz?

A) Read the quotes on the previous page. Find:

    a) three that contain spelling mistakes

    b) one that is more ridiculous than all the others

    c) two that state the obvious

    d) one that reveals that the candidate was probably using a template

    e) two that show that the candidate has a giant ego

B) Below are two drafts of the same personal statement. The student, from France (and not a native English speaker) had been asked by a university in the UK to write "a statement regarding why you wish to study the Film Studies side of the programme and the areas that most interest you in this subject area." What are the main differences between the first and final drafts.

FIRST DRAFT

I want to study cinema because I'm fascinated by how every angle and framing can have a precise meaning, how every choice has a particular importance, channeling an idea into a fragment of a few seconds. I'm keen to observe carefully and then reflect on what I see, for this reason I believe that the structure of your course offers me the best opportunity to express and fortify my critical approach and skills in film studies and film making. My aim is to become a director engaged in social issues, therefore I'm convinced that studying in a multicultural country will allow me to find my own film making style and explore my boundaries and values, key points in the personality of an artist. I'm willing to deepen my knowledge of the history of cinema because I find extraordinary how a society has manifested its changes through cinema and film. It is my firm conviction that a logical approach, communication and a solid technique are fundamental to be able to support the creative inspiration with the required ability to portray a concept at its fullest potential, to develop its sensations and intentions. I would be grateful to take part in your program because I'm enthusiastic to grow and give my personal contribution to the world of cinema. Your university would certainly offer the possibility to acquire a solid technique in order to increase my artistic possibilities.

FINAL DRAFT

I am keen to study cinema because I'm fascinated by how every angle and frame can have a precise meaning, how every choice has a particular importance. I'm particularly interested in the representation of concepts and opinions through cinema, because this can help us understand and show the real evolution of modern societies, questioning contemporary values and points of view.

5.1 What's the buzz? (cont.)

What most interests me about your film program is the combination of both analysis and practice, because I'm keen to think critically, and work pragmatically to articulate my thoughts about an issue. For example, I was one of the organizers of my school film club, where I personally interviewed local directors about their work and after class discussions me and my friends would try to create our own short films, guided by some professional experts from our region of France. In the course that I did with the French director and actor axe, I had the opportunity to direct with him a scene that I had previously written, with actors and a cameraman.

I am very keen to deepen my knowledge of the history of cinema because I find it extraordinary how a society has manifested its changes, needs and opinions through cinematography. For example, I was raised watching the society I lived in express its cultural and social development through French cinema, which has always played a great part in my artistic view. I'm convinced that at your university I will be able to compare French cinema with cinematography from other countries and study the different structures.

Finally, I hope my experiences in France will be of interest to my fellow students. I believe that studying in a multicultural environment will allow me not only to find my own film making style but also to explore my boundaries and values.

In this chapter you will learn what a personal statement, a motivational letter and a statement of interest are. You will be given tips on how to write and structure an academic biography in short and extended versions, and in a version for a home page.

5.2   What is a Personal Statement? What are the elements of a good Personal Statement?

A personal statement is an optional section, typically written by candidates who have finished their education with a normal degree without doing an MSc, a PhD or a post-doc qualification.

Personal statements (generally of a maximum of 4000 characters) are also used by school leavers when applying to university.

The aim of a personal statement is to show that you:

- have the right qualifications for the place / position you are seeking

- have the right skills - both technical and personal (i.e. soft skills)

- can describe yourself and your achievements concisely

Below is a personal statement written by a young British graduate who wishes to secure a job in teaching English as a foreign language (TEFL) in a language school. It highlights some of the good and bad points of a typical personal statement.

Personal Statement:

Having a BSc degree has given me the skills required to use language to a high standard and write and communicate with many different people. Among the modules I studied were:

- Environmental Management

- Environmental Law

- Information Technology and Quantitative Biology

- Environmental Economics

I have worked primarily in the customer services area either in shops or on a campsite, which has given me good experience of working with people in teams and offering an appropriate quality of service to customers. I have completed a TEFL course in order to teach English; completing this course has helped my skills in planning, listening, speaking to groups, and ensuring understanding. Since then I have undertaken more teaching qualifications and employment all of which have been very successful; I have been well received by students, fellow teachers and course organisers. Recently I have been more and more involved in TEFL teaching having been working both in my home city of Bristol and in Prague. I would really like to extend these experiences to working abroad, especially in your city, to which I have a particular attachment having enjoyed my stay previously.

I am committed to finding for myself a career, but I need an opportunity. I hope than you will give me an opportunity to start a career with you and within the industry.

5.2 What is a Personal Statement? What are the elements of a good Personal Statement? (cont.)

Her layout is clear using bullet points, she clearly lists the main topics she studied at university and she tries to connect this to TEFL by saying that she has strong skills in writing and communicating. However there are a number of problems:

- the statement is very long, although she claims to have good writing and communication skills, his statement shows that she is prone to repetition and redundancy. She says she has completed a TEFL course and then adds *in order to teach English* - this is redundant given the fact that the TE in TEFL stands for 'teaching English', the same redundancy is in 'TEFL teaching'. However, this tactic of repeating her key words (i.e. TEFL, teaching and English), means that if she submitted an electronic version of her CV to a recruiting agency website, it might stand a better chance of being picked up during any automatic screening process of CVs
- the statement does not seem to have been tailored specifically for the reader - she says *especially in your city*. If she is writing directly to a language school, she would be better to write the exact location of the language school and mention the exact time she visited that town, rather than writing something so generic that gives the idea that she has probably never even been to *your city*. Moreover, the fact that she used *your city* shows that she hasn't really made an effort, and this could be interpreted by the reader that she would be happy to work in any city
- in her final paragraph, she sounds a little desperate (*I need an opportunity*) and also the phrase *I am committed to finding for myself a caree*r sounds a little strange, given that securing a career is the objective of most graduates. Again it sounds like she may be applying for jobs in any field, not the specific field of TEFL

Below is a revised version. The main differences with respect to the original version are highlighted in italics.

Personal Statement:

My BSc has provided me with the skills required to use language to a high standard and write and communicate with many different people. Among the modules I studied were:

- Environmental Management
- Environmental Law
- Information Technology and Quantitative Biology
- Environmental Economics

5.2 What is a Personal Statement? What are the elements of a good Personal Statement? (cont.)

I have worked primarily in the customer services area both in *shops and campsites*. *This* has given me valuable experience of working with people in teams and offering an appropriate quality of service to customers.

During my TEFL course I further improved my skills in planning, listening, speaking to groups, and ensuring understanding. Since then I have *acquired* more teaching qualifications and *have successfully gained additional teaching experience in my home town of Bristol and in Prague. As testified by the attached references,* I have been well received by students, fellow teachers and course organisers.

I would really like to extend these experiences to working abroad, *especially in Moscow*, to which I have a particular attachment - *my maternal grandmother was born in a village near Moscow.*

I very much look forward to having an opportunity to meet you.

The revised version:

- is 20% shorter. All the repetition and redundancy has been removed, but no content has been lost

- has more paragraphs - this makes it easier to read

- has removed ambiguity (e.g. *acquired* teaching qualifications, rather than *undertaken* - *undertaken* sounds like the courses were started but not completed)

- mentions *references* to give her more credibility, i.e. what she says can be supported by the people she has worked for

- mentions the specific city where she wants to work (Moscow) rather than saying *your city* (this generic use of *your city* could indicate to the recruiter that the candidate has sent the same personal statement to lots of English language schools. A tailored personal statement has more impact

- has deleted the rather strange final paragraph

The combination of the above changes makes the statement sound as if the candidate had put a lot of effort into creating it. It also sounds makes the candidate sound more dynamic.

5.2 What is a Personal Statement? What are the elements of a good Personal Statement? (cont.)

Note: Don't confuse a Personal Statement with a Research Statement. A research statement is a summary of research achievements and a proposal for upcoming research. It includes BOTH current aims and findings AND future goals. How to write a research statement is outside the scope of this book, but useful information can be found here:

https://gradschool.cornell.edu/academic-progress/pathways-to-success/prepare-for-your-career/take-action/research-statement/

https://www.psychologicalscience.org/observer/how-to-write-a-research-statement

5.3 What is a motivational letter? What is a statement of interest?

There is no real difference in the aim of a cover letter, motivational letter or a statement of interest. All of them are opportunities for you to expand upon some of the more salient and interesting points of your CV and to interpret their significance for the HR person.

These letters are a way for you to sound dynamic and really differentiate yourself from other candidates. Your letter should answer such question as: What targets did you reach? How well did the projects go? What did you learn from them? How could this experience be applied to the position you are applying for?

From an employer's point of view, these letters / statements are demonstrations of

- how much you care about getting the job
- your writing ability
- your attention to detail
- your communication skills

The key differences are that a motivational letter or a statement of interest tends:

- not to be in response to a specific job advertisement
- to be used in academia rather than business
- to be longer than a cover letter

There is no real difference between *motivational letter* and *statement of interest* - they mean the same thing.

So, if a research institute or university requests a motivational letter or a statement of interest, you can follow all the suggestions in the rest of this chapter, but simply provide more details. This means that you are likely to write more than one page of text.

5.4   What is a bio? When would I need one?

A bio is a biography, i.e. the story of a person's life, or in the context of this book, their academic career.

A 4-5 line bio might also be called 'About' on a university webpage or social media site. Bios are typically used by people in academia and research, for:

- Conferences. If you are giving a presentation at an international conference, the organizers may ask you for a short summary of your career and major achievements. The organizers will then use this bio for the conference proceedings.

- Books and book chapters. If you are asked to contribute to a publication, you may be requested to provide a bio.

- Grant applications

- Your personal home page or blog, or your institute's home page.

- Social/professional networking sites, including Twitter

Bios are typically read by:

- colleagues/academics in your department or discipline

- undergraduate students in your department who may be taking a course with you

- academics in other fields who may be attending the same conference as you

- potential employees

If you place a bio on your home page (either your personal one or your institutes), you may consider using more than one format:

- 'About' - where you describe in a couple of sentences who you are: name, position, department, institute, research interests.

- 'Short academic bio' - where you provide in the first person a brief summary of your academic career and experience. This will be slightly more detailed than the 'About', e.g. you might present a short list of your research interests..

- 'Extended academic bio' - where you write in the third person (or with no pronouns) more details your academic career experience, and research interests. Here you will mentioned your degree(s), projects, award, publications. An example is given in the next subsection.

- 'CV' - in this case you simply provide a link to your full CV

By providing several versions of the same info you can let your 'audience' (colleagues, undergraduates, conference goes etc) choose what kind of information they are interested in.

5.5   What is the structure of an extended bio?

Bios for both conference proceedings and books tend to be written in a very formal way using the third person (i.e. *he / she, his / her*). They are usually structured as one paragraph.

Typical things to mention include:

1. your degree(s)

2. previous positions

3. your current position

4. what projects you have worked on

5. what project you are working on now

6. your plans for the future

7. the number of first author publications

8. the number of conferences attended where you gave a presentation

9. committees that you are on

10. patents held

Things that you might write on your CV but probably would not include in your bio are:

- non technical skills

- teaching experience

- private interests

Below is an example. The numbers in square brackets correspond to points 1-10 above.

[1] Volmar Thorgaard holds a degree in physics from the University of Copenhagen, Denmark. [2] In 2024 he joined KNUT, an institute of the Danish National Research Council. Starting in early 2026, he spent 18 months at the IBM Scientific Center in Cambridge, Massachusetts, working on computer networks. [4] He has since directed several national and international projects including (in chronological order): xxx, yyy, zzz. [3] In 2028 he joined the Department of Information Engineering of the University of Helsinki, where he is now an assistant professor. [5] His current research interests include the design and performance evaluation of PMAC protocols for wireless networks and quality of service provision in integrated and differentiated services networks. [6] He is planning to bring together Scandinavian countries into a joint project linking up research center computers to Finland's space station on Mars. [7] Thorgaard is the first author of 10 papers published in international journals, [8] and has presented his research at all the major conferences on technologies for Mars in the last decade. [9] He is on the editorial committee for the two top space technology journals in Scandinavia. [10] He is co-author of several patents with Danish Telecom and Nokia, in the areas of scheduling algorithms.

5.5 What is the structure of an extended bio? (cont.)

Note the following:

- Volmar avoids beginning every sentence with *he* by occasionally beginning with a date, using *his*, and using his name (both his full name, and his family name alone)

- present simple to refer to present situations: ***holds*** *a degree in physics,* ***is*** *co-author of several patents*;

- present perfect for situations that began in the past and are still true today (Volmar still directs projects): *he* ***has*** ***since*** ***directed*** *several national and international projects*

- past simple for finished actions: *In 2028 he* ***joined*** *the Department of Information Engineering*

5.6 How do I write a bio for a home page?

For their personal home page, people generally use the first person (i.e. *I, my*). For the home page of their university or research institute both personal and impersonal forms are used, and the choice depends on how formal you wish to be.

Below is an example from a researcher's personal home page.

I am a postdoctoral fellow at the European Space Agency and a visitor in physics with Caltech.

My primary research interest is the observation of astrophysically unmodeled bursts of gravitational waves from sources such as core collapse supernovae, the merger of binary compact objects, the progenitors of gamma-ray bursts, or perhaps unanticipated sources. In particular, I am interested in taking advantage of the new global network of interferometric gravitational wave observatories, composed of the LIGO detectors in the US and the GEO and Virgo detectors in Europe, in order to maximize the prospects for detection and the physics that we can learn.

I currently live in Pisa, Italy, and work at the nearby European Gravitational Observatory.

For a list of publications, please see my curriculum vitae (pdf).

Note how she structures her bio into several paragraphs:

1. current position
2. current interests and aspirations
3. indication of where she lives and where she works
4. reference to a pdf version of her CV and list of publications

You also need to give all your contact details.

Note also how she:

- uses the first person pronoun (i.e. *I, my*) but still maintains quite a formal style
- inserts a lot of key technical words - this should increase her chances of being found by a search engine
- is very succinct, she only gives essential information - she doesn't waste the reader's time with unnecessary words or information

5.7 Can my academic biography include personal information and humor?

Some researchers like to provide some personal information in their bio as can provide insights into the personality and work style that could not otherwise be gleaned from a simple list of academic qualifications and achievements.

Others also like to include a little humor. If you are not a native speaker and thus do not have an excellent command of the nuances of the English language, then including humor can be risky as what you may think is funny, may not be funny to others and may even appear offensive. So always have your bio (and CV, and any other important document) checked by a native speaker with experience in writing academic documents.

Below is the short academic biography for Professor Dan Grossman, which at the time of my search on Google was the top-ranking bio. Professor Grossman kindly gave me permission to use it. I think it is a great bio.

The bio is written in the third person (*Dan, he, his*) and is structured as follows (the numbers refer to the paragraphs).

1. key info about his current role

2. educational background

3. other activities - committee work

4. other activities - teaching work

5. personal info + humor

6. humor (unexpected info revealing that Professor Grossman must be a fun character)

The penultimate paragraph also provide readers with information that they could use on a social occasion if they happened to meet Dan at a conference.

Dan Grossman is a Professor in the Paul G. Allen School of Computer Science & Engineering at the University of Washington where he has been a faculty member since 2003. He holds the J. Ray Bowen Professorship for Innovation in Engineering Education. He is the Allen School's Deputy Director.

Dan completed his Ph.D. at Cornell University and his undergraduate studies at Rice University. His research interests lie in the area of programming languages, ranging from theory to design to implementation. He has collaborated actively with researchers in several other disciplines of computer science, particularly computer architecture on problems at the hardware/software interface.

5.7   Can my academic biography include personal information and humor? (cont.)

Dan has served on roughly thirty conference and workshop program committees and is the Program Chair for PLDI 2018. He has served on the ACM SIGPLAN Executive Committee, the Steering Committee for the ACM / IEEE-CS 2013 Computer Science Curriculum, and the ACM Education Board. He currently serves on the CRA Board.

Dan is the instructor for a popular MOOC on undergraduate topics in programming languages and functional programming.

Dan lives with his partner, an international public-health researcher, their two sons, born December 2013 and September 2015, and, because that clearly isn't enough chaos, a puppy born October 2016. Prior to becoming a proud and obsessed dad, Dan enjoyed playing (poorly) and watching ice hockey, (road) bicycling, hiking, non-fiction, and enjoying good food, beer, and live theatre. Now he usually manages to read one book a month.

Dan has never had a cavity.

https://homes.cs.washington.edu/~djg/grossman_bio.html by kind permission of Professor Dan Grossman

5.8   How should I report my publications?

If you are applying for a job in research or academia, and the main part of your CV is looking full, you could put your Publications on a separate page. Alternatively, you can locate it directly under either 'Other skills' or 'Hobbies and interests'.

You might also consider dividing up your publications into the following subsections:

- *Selected Refereed Publications* - these are the ones you want the reader to focus on

- *Other Refereed Publications* - these extra ones help to highlight the quantity of research that you have had published

- *Pending Publications* - these are ones that either you have submitted (and are awaiting confirmation) or that are currently at the press

- *Technical Notes* - these are short articles outlining a specific development / modification, technique or procedure

You should list your publications in the same way as you would normally list the publications at the end of a paper. With regard to pending publications you can write:

A. Wallwork et al. "Detailed comparison of word order in Modern and Old English". To appear in Annals of Ling. Rev.

A. Wallwork et al. "The subjunctive in Old English texts". Submitted to Int. Lang. Rev.

The term *to appear in* means that your paper has already been accepted for publication, whereas *submitted to* means you are waiting for the outcome.

If you are applying for a job in industry, you don't need to have a list of publications or a separate section dedicated to publications.

However, the fact that you have published your research is still important, even to an employer in industry. Publishing your work means that you have certain skills:

- writing in English about technical matters

- communicating with referees and editors, so you will have written many formal emails and letters

- meeting deadlines

- presenting your paper / research at international conferences

5.8 How should I report my publications? (cont.)

So the solution is to add a short subsection to your Education or Work Experience section in which you write something like this:

First author of five papers on civil engineering, published in international journals. Presented three of these papers at international conferences. Papers available at: www.blahblah/blah

5.9 Do's and Don'ts: Writing a Bio

Be concise, accurate and factual.

Do mention:

- your academic qualifications
- previous and current positions
- previous, present and future projects
- publications and conferences
- committees, patents and awards

Style

- third person (i.e. *he/she developed* rather than *I developed*) for conferences and book chapters
- first person for home pages

Chapter 6
Education

Factoids: Women in Science

NOBEL PRIZES: Between 1901 and 1960 a woman received a Nobel Prize on average once every 4.2 years; 1961-2000 once every 2.4 years; and since 2000 every 0.75 years.

CHINA: When Yingying Lu, Ph.D., was made a professor at the College of Chemical & Biological Engineering at Zhejiang University, she was only 27 years old and possibly the youngest professor (male or female) in the world. Between 43% and 52% of teachers at higher education institutes in China are female.

IRAN VS UK: The total populations of Iran and the UK are approximately 65 million and 78 million respectively, yet there are more than twice as many female university students in Iran than in the UK (2.1 million vs 0.9 million).

JAPAN: An investigation into a top medical school found that in the 2018 entrance exams the school had reduced all applicants' first-stage test scores by 20% and then added at least 20 points for male applicants. Similar manipulations had occurred for years because the school wanted fewer female doctors claiming they would shorten or terminate their careers after becoming mothers.

KOREA: More than 75% of Korean girls go to university. Yi So-yeon was the first Korean woman to go into space and is probably Korea's most famous female scientist.

LATVIA: Holds the world record for the highest share of women amongst scientific staff and the highest share of women with a PhD (Latvia 60%, USA 53%, Germany 45%)

SPAIN: Approximately 1:3 of researchers are women, less than 20% of women hold a high position. 18% of Spanish women aged 55-64 hold a university degree or PhD, this rises to 47.5% for those aged between 25 and 34.

UK: The first man to graduate from Cambridge University was in 1209, the first woman in 1948. The first man to be made a fellow at the Royal Society (the oldest scientific institute in the world) was in 1600, the first woman in 1946.

USA: There are more females graduates with a bachelor's degree in health professions (85% women, 15% men), public administration, education, psychology and languages than there are in math and statistics, architecture, physical sciences, computer science, engineering (83% men, 17% women).

© Springer Nature Switzerland AG 2019
A. Wallwork, *English for Academic CVs, Resumes, and Online Profiles*,
English for Academic Research, https://doi.org/10.1007/978-3-030-11090-1_6

6.1   What's the buzz?

A) Look at the factoids on the previous page, most of which appeared in my book *English for Presentations at International Conferences*. Decide which fact you find most surprising and discuss the situation of women in education in your country.

B) To what extent do you think the following quotation from 1881 is still true today: *Let the 'environment' of women be similar to that of men and with his opportunities, before she be fairly judged, intellectually his inferior, please.* Caroline Kennard, an American amateur scientist and advocate of women's rights.

C) Discuss the questions.

In your country ...

- How long does a typical degree last?
- At what age do people generally finish university?
- Is a Master's worth the expense?
- What are the most difficult aspects of doing a PhD?
- Which is the best university in your country?
- What kind of job are you looking for - a) academia b) industry?
- What do you want from a job? In terms of the specific type of job - list three essential requirements and three desirable (but not essential) attributes.

Which <u>one</u> of the following is the most important for you:

- ❑ to put into practice what you learned during university
- ❑ to learn new skills
- ❑ to work with friendly and like-minded colleagues with similar interests
- ❑ to work autonomously

If you want to work in academia / research:

- should the research institute be (a) state-funded or (b) private
- should it be in a (a) small or (b) large town
- in (a) your country or (b) abroad
- focused on (a) what you studied at university or on (b) a different research area

6.1 What's the buzz? (cont.)

If you want to work in industry, ideally for you which <u>one</u> of the following should the company be:

- ❑ a start up
- ❑ a large well-established company in your own country
- ❑ a small to medium sized company
- ❑ a multinational

This chapter explains whether you need to structure your education and work experience sections to make it seem as if you have always been following a well-defined path. You will learn how to lay out the education section, what to include, what style to adopt (personal or impersonal), and where to locate it within your CV.

6.2 Should I make my education and work experience look as if I have always been following a well-defined path?

Your CV has a primary aim - to get you a specific job. In a sense your CV is like a proposal - you are making a case that you are the right candidate for a specific job. What you write in your Work Experience and Education sections should focus on the information needed to support your case. This information will include:

- academic qualifications and grades

- special activities or projects that could be seen as relevant for the job you are looking for

- research studies that match the job description

- experience in other labs or work placements that are relevant for the lab / institute / company where you want to work

However this does not mean that you should focus exclusively on what you consider to be relevant information. Even if your CV does not portray a totally coherent career path, this is not important. If you have done other activities or changed course at some points, this is only human and could be interpreted as a good sign that you have a broad experience and are not afraid to try out new areas. Also, you cannot know exactly what your potential employer is looking for, and some of your supposedly 'irrelevant' experiences might actually be relevant to the employer or might reveal an aspect of your character that the employer sees as being useful.

6.3 Where should the Education and Work sections be located?

If you finished your education several years ago, the Education section should appear after your Work Experience section and should contain fewer details than in the Work Experience section.

If you have just finished or are currently finishing your education, then you are unlikely to have had much work experience, so the Education section should appear before the Work section.

The sections on education and work should include the:

- start and end dates; everything should be in reverse chronological order

- name and location of the institute / place of work

- type of degree / position at work

- brief details of coursework / your role at work

6.4 What is the typical layout?

Below is a typical layout.

	Education and training
2028-2031	PhD (ISCED 6), funded by an Economic and Social Research Council Award at Brunel University, London, UK
	Thesis Title: 'Young People in the Construction of the Virtual University', empirical research that directly contributes to debates on e-learning.
2024-2027	Bachelor of Science in Sociology and Psychology (ISCED 5), Brunel University, London, UK.
	Principal subjects/occupational skills covered: Sociology of Risk, Sociology of Scientific Knowledge/ Information Society; E-learning and Psychology; Research Methods.

Here is an alternative layout. Note how:

- the information is in reverse chronological order - this is mandatory in a CV

- the candidate has begun directly with her university education

- the candidate got her BSc in Bolivia and has also indicated how long the course was (5 years) - this is important as it shows that her course was longer than the standard 3-year course

- she has just written her thesis titles, without describing any details - this is because in both cases her thesis title is self-explanatory

Education

2026 - 2028 University of Manchester, UK

Doctor of Philosophy in Information Engineering

Research in greening the Internet. Elective coursework included: enhanced Internet architecture employing advanced communication service paradigms, protocols and algorithms targeted at the optimization of energy consumption. Dissertation "A radical energy-aware application for wireless energy reduction" advised by Professor Giuseppe Verdi.

2023-2050 University of Santiago, Chile

Bachelor of Science degree (5 year course) in Electrical Engineering

Engineering coursework included: continuous and discrete systems and signal processing, analog and digital circuit design, and computational theory. Undergraduate thesis project, "Wireless Enabled Context Awareness for the Future Internet".

6.5 Which is better *I developed a system* or *Developed a system* (i.e. with or without the personal pronoun)?

You can used verbs without a subject at the beginning of each bullet point (e.g. *secured, architected, developed, controlled*). Instead, if the verb does not come at the beginning of the bullet point, then you would probably use the personal pronoun before the noun (highlighted in italics in the example below):

As part of this project, *I developed* a Java stream processing application running on the S5 platform for detecting algorithmically generated domain names in DNS queries. *I also standardized* procedures regarding 'Scalable and Elastic Event Processing' (SEEP) and <u>secured</u> applications by enforcing Information Flow Control policies within middleware.

Note that the verb underlined (*secured*) has no subject as it is implicit because it is within the same sentence as *I also standardized*.

Resumes tend to avoid the use of personal pronouns (highlighted in italics below).

As part of this project, *was responsible for the development* of a Java stream processing application running on the S5 platform for detecting algorithmically generated domain names in DNS queries. Also, *was in charge of setting up* standardized procedures regarding 'Scalable and Elastic Event Processing' (SEEP) and ...

6.6 How should I write the date in the Work Experience and Education sections?

Normally the year will suffice:

2020

2020-2022

2023 - present

You only need to write the month in two cases.

1. if it refers to a very recent date (i.e. of this year, or the end of the previous year). For example, if we are now in May 2029, you might write this range of dates to describe an internship: *Jun 2028 - Mar 2029*. All months are abbreviated with the first three letters: May, Jun, July etc.

2. if the period of time was very short and goes from the end of one year to the beginning of the next year:

Nov 2024 - Jan 2025

The way you write dates affects the overall appearance of your CV, as you can see from the example from the Education section. These examples are non standard, and thus give the appearance of a lack of consistency in your CV, which could easily be interpreted as a lack of organization in your working habits:

BAD EXAMPLE

- ○ 2020-2022: Erasmus student at the University of Turku, Finland.
- ○ M.A. in Language Science at the University Ca' Foscari of Venice, Italy, 2023.
- ○ Since October 2025 - PhD student in Cognitive Sciences at the University of Siena, Italy.

The example above is bad because:

- The dates are <u>not</u> in reverse chronological order.
- The dates appear both at the beginning and the end of the sentences, so they are difficult to locate.
- In addition to looking messy, the problem is that the way the dates have been written does not conform to the standard way of writing dates. This will not be appreciated by recruiters.

6.7   I am not sure whether my degree has an equivalent outside my own country. What should I do?

Every country has its own system of naming and classifying degrees. On Wikipedia there are full descriptions of the types of degree (Bachelor's, Master's, PhD) you can obtain in the UK and the USA.

The equivalents between first degrees in the UK and the USA are listed in table below, which comes from the University College London website (www.ucl.ac.uk/).

UK	USA / Canada
First-class Honors	GPA (grade point average) 3.6/4.0
Upper second-class Honors	GPA 3.3/4.0
Lower second-class Honors	GPA 3.0/4.0

When you list your academic qualifications it may be worth trying to explain what your degree is equivalent to in the country where you are sending your CV. For example, imagine you have done your first degree in Mexico and you have decided to send your CV to two institutes: one in the USA and one in Germany. You can look on Wikipedia to see what is the closest equivalent to your Mexican degree, and you will discover that it is called a Bachelor's (http://en.wikipedia.org/wiki/Bachelor's_degree). You then look for descriptions of Bachelor's degrees in the USA and Germany. Obviously, you will write two CVs, one for each country. On the one for the USA, you can describe your degree by using a direct equivalent for the score you got.

2024-2029	Bachelor of Science in Telecommunications, Universidad Nacional Autónoma de México - score: 98/100 cum laude (equivalent to GPA 4.0)

To prepare the CV for Germany you can look at Wikipedia's entry for Germany (http://en.wikipedia.org/wiki/Bachelor's_degree#Germany) where you will discover that the name of your degree in German is either *Bakkalaureus* or *Bachelor* and that in Germany this requires three years of study. But maybe your degree lasted five years, so in this case you need to state the difference in length.

2024-2029	Bachelor of Science in Telecommunications, Universidad Nacional Autónoma de México - score: 98/100 cum laude (equivalent to *Bachelor* in Germany, note: the duration of the course was 5 years)

If you are unable to find an equivalent to your degree, then you could also put a link next to your qualification to a website where there is a full description of your degree in English. Note: in the example below the website is fictional.

6.7 I am not sure whether my degree has an equivalent outside my own country. What should I do? (cont.)

2020-2021	Master's in Particle Physics (full description at http://english.pku.edu.cn/blahblah), University of Bejing, China

The Bologna Process aims to have a common description of degrees / standards inside Europe, see http://en.wikipedia.org/wiki/Bologna_Process.

6.8   What about additional courses that I have attended?

In addition to your main degree courses, you may wish to include other courses that you attended that are pertinent to the job you are applying for and which would be beneficial to the position you are seeking.

Below is an example from a recent graduate:

Manchester Academy of English – CELTA (Pass)

The course focused on: x, y, z. It highlighted the importance of seeing things from the learner's perspective in order to gain insights into how best to teach English. We undertook six hours of assessed teaching practice, observed six hours' worth of experienced teachers' lessons, and completed four assignments. Studying for the course part-time whilst holding down two jobs vastly improved my time-management skills and taught me how to manage my workload effectively.

Note how he does not merely say what the course consisted of (*x, y and z*) but also the benefit for the candidate (*importance of seeing* ...). He takes the opportunity to show how the fact that he did the course and worked at the same time highlights that he now has particular skills (*time management*) that will be relevant for the job he is applying for.

He uses a personal style throughout. If you choose to adopt such a style, then be very careful as you are more likely to make errors in English.

6.9   Education: Do's and Don'ts

➤ The correct term for this section is *Education* not *Formation*.

➤ Do put your achievements in reverse chronological order. What are you doing now is generally considered more important than what you did in the past.

➤ If you finished your education after your first degree and are now looking for your first job, then putting your high school is perfectly normal and accept-able. However, if you subsequently did a Master's or PhD then mentioning your school is probably not necessary.

➤ Only put your score (for tests and degrees) if the score will make sense to someone who has not been through your country's education system. In any case interpret the score for your readers. For example, if scores in your country are recorded as a percentage then you could write that you obtained a score of 89% and that a score of between 85%-90% is only achieved by one in twenty students. This then gives the reader an idea of how good you are.

➤ Only put your thesis title if it is self-explanatory. If it is not self explanatory, you can write, for example:

Thesis on new methodologies for extracting gold from recycled plastic. The pro-cedure involved three steps ...

In any case the description of your thesis should not be more than two lines long.

➤ There is no need to write the exact date you defended you thesis (unless this is very recent).

➤ Do not write anything that is not true. Do not change dates to show that there are no gaps. Instead explain the gaps in your cover letter.

➤ Do not put the exact day and month of your graduation / thesis. Just write the year. If you graduated very recently: the month and year.

➤ Abbreviate months (but not years). The official abbreviations use the first three letters: Jan, Feb, Mar, Apr, May, Jun, Jul, Aug, Sep, Oct, Nov, Dec. Good exam-ples: Nov 2020 - Feb 2021   May - Jun 2023   Oct 2024

➤ Do not invent your own abbreviations for months. You do not need to use a period (.) at the end of the abbreviation.

Chapter 7
Work / Research Experience

Factoids

❖ In the UK around 1 in 3 students and graduates 'embellish' their CVs: 11% falsely claimed to hold a degree, 40% had inflated their grade.

❖ Employers who do not cross check job applications from jobseekers have a one in three chance of employing unqualified staff, potentially putting the business at risk of fraudulent, dishonest or inappropriate behavior. A survey revealed that almost a third of CVs from job hunters contained discrepancies relating to professional qualifications and memberships, ranging them being out of date to not been held at all.

❖ Studies have shown that 95% of US college students are willing to lie to get a job.

❖ A survey conducted by Experian revealed that 37% of job seekers had lied about their previous experience, 21% lied about their qualifications, and 19% had not been honest about their current salaries.

❖ A student from Yale once submitted a video version of his CV to the financial services firm UBS. The seven-minute film was forwarded to every investment in Wall Street with subject lines such as "What NOT to do when looking for a banking job".

❖ A 12-year study of the career paths of over 650 business professionals revealed that one of the most common mistakes in choosing a career was basing choices on aptitudes rather than interests.

❖ In a survey by Powerchex, a UK pre-employment screening company, discrepancies were found in 43% of the job application forms of students from low-ranking UK universities (14% in top universities).

❖ Before employing someone, companies may use a professional third party to cross check the candidates qualifications and experiences, also by looking for consistency between what is stated in their CV and what it says, for instance, on their LinkedIn or Research Gate profile, even on their Facebook page.

© Springer Nature Switzerland AG 2019
A. Wallwork, *English for Academic CVs, Resumes, and Online Profiles*,
English for Academic Research, https://doi.org/10.1007/978-3-030-11090-1_7

7.1 What's the buzz?

A) Discuss the following.

1. Which are three most difficult professions to get into:

   a) space exploration b) the music business c) an advertising agency creative department d) judge in a high court e) computer software engineer

2. What do the jobs below have in common?

   kitchen porter, waitress, catering assistant, laundry worker, supermarket shelf-filler, cleaner/domestic, bar staff, childcarer, retail check-out operator, hairdresser

3. Which three of the following perks would you most like to have at work?

   six month sabbatical every 15 years, b) use of company plane for family emergencies, c) 24 hour fitness center for workers and families, d) 50% discount on all company products and services, e) free subscription to Netflix, f) free massages, g) free lunch and dinner, h) four-weeks unpaid leave per year to do whatever you want

4. Which of these jobs may actually make the world a worse place?

   a) lawyers b) accountants working in mergers and acquisitions c) politicians

5. In which of these fields are people most likely to say their job is highly meaningful?

   a) clergy b) military c) education d) media e) sports f) sales g) social services

6. Which of the following are not 'acceptable' practices at work?

   a) going on Facebook b) flirting with colleagues c) regularly taking extra long lunch breaks d) clocking in for someone else e) taking home office stationery

7.1   What's the buzz? (cont.)

B) According to researchers at the University of Hertfordshire, whether you are successful comes down to the specific words and phrases used on your form. Look at the 20 words below and decide which 10 should be avoided.

○ Achievement	○ Developed	○ Impact	○ Nothing
○ Active	○ Evidence	○ Individual	○ Panic
○ Always	○ Experience	○ Involved	○ Planning
○ Awful	○ Fault	○ Mistake	○ Problems
○ Bad	○ Hate	○ Never	○ Transferable skills

In this chapter you will find the answers to questions such as: *How should I lay out the Work Experience section? How can I make my key words stand out, yet not be too obtrusive? How should I describe internships and other research experiences? How can I highlight how my work experience fits in with the post I am applying for? What key words should I try to insert?* You will also learn how to deal with 'jobs' that don't immediately seem to fit under the heading 'Work Experience'.

Note: The Work Experience section has many similarities with the Education section. See the following sections in Chapter 6 Education:

- where to locate the Work Experience section (6.3)

- whether the Work Experience section should give the idea of a logical progression in your career (6.2)

- use or not of personal pronouns in the description of what roles you carried out (6.5)

7.2 How should I lay out the Work Experience section?

You can lay out this section in exactly the same way as the Education section (see 6.4).

Below are some examples that, unlike the examples in Chapter 6, are not based on the Europass.

EXAMPLE 1 The candidate below has organized her Work Experience in their CV as follows:

- first line: dates + name of company

- second line: her position within the company

- bullet points: each indicating key roles that she carried out

The amount of detail depends on how much space you have available.

2026 - present: Zed Engineering Group, Kuala Lumpur
Principal Engineer – Secure Systems

- Secured $500,000 of funding for research into MegaData stream processing architectures. As part of this project, I developed a Java stream processing application running on the S5 platform for detecting algorithmically generated domain names in DNS queries. I also standardized procedures regarding 'Scalable and Elastic Event Processing' (SEEP) and secured applications by enforcing Information Flow Control policies within middleware.

- Architected and developed innovative security architecture, wrriten in core Java, for a test-bed sharing coalition Intelligence, Surveillance and Reconnaissance data at different classifications.

2020 - 2026: Tata Engineering, automotive depatment
Software Architect

- Controlled the software architecture for real-time embedded systems in the Driver Information product line.

- Reviewed work products: implementing critical features (using object-oriented C and Java), Specifying the development methiodology and processes, and troubleshooting problems.

- Supported new business wins with major car manufactures.

EXAMPLE 2 This is from a one-page resume in two columns. It only contains essential information. Note the very clear layout and minimal use of punctuation

Work Experience	Languages
Transdence (2026-present)	*Spanish – Native Speaker*
DE-EN Interpreter for Expert Network Calls	*English – Native Speaker*
	TOEFL-ITP 670 Points (2025)
English proofreader and editor	Trinity College London -ISE III
	German –C2 CEFR
	Münchner Volkshochschule (2017-2018)

7.3 Do I have to call this section *Work Experience*? Are there any other alternatives?

If you are in the field of research, you may not consider your research experiences as classifiable under work. Below are three examples with an alternative title. They also highlight a different format from the ones given in 7.2.

EXAMPLE 1

CURRENT RESEARCH SUBMITTED AND IN PREPARATION

2028 - now	**Swiss National Research Council**
	• Research and development of DNA sensor based on capacitive monitoring
	• Investigation on smart scaffold for cell growth sensing
2026 - 2028	**Mechancial Engineering Department - University of Indonesia**
	• Research and development of Mini/Micro Direct Methanol Fuel Cell
	• Nanofludis Stabilization for Heat transfer Medium
	• Electroplating Process Based on Turbulence Controlled of Mass Transferred
2024 - 2025	**Forschungszentrum Juelich GmBh, Germany**
	Institute for Energy and process Engineering - Fuel Cell Project
	• Membrane Electrode Assembly (MEA) Improvement
2021 - 2024	**Chemical Engineering Department - Gadjah Mada University, Indonesia**
	• Developing a mathematical modeling for kerosene extraction in a continuous column
	• Modelling of SO3 conversion in H2SO4 plant at PT Petrokimia Gresik, IND.

EXAMPLE 2

Projects	Design of RAMHORMOZ diversion dam in southern Iran.
	Flood plain and flood control systems design for the river Karun.
	Determination of density current in DEZ dam.
	Investigation into sediment budget and sediment balance for the river Karun.
	Rivers and Reservoirs Bathymetry.

7.3 Do I have to call this section *Work Experience*? Are there any other alternatives? (cont.)

EXAMPLE 3

Research   UNIVERSITY OF ROME, LA SAPIENZA   Cascina, Italy
Experience   *December 2006 - present*

Postdoctoral fellow
Recipient of an Italian Istituto Nazionale di Fisica Nucleare (INFN) postdoctoral fellowship to perform research at the Virgo gravitational-wave detector near Pisa, Italy. Research focused on the development of coherent analysis methods for the detection, validation, and recovery of gravitational-wave bursts in data from the new global network of interferometric gravitational-wave detectors.

CALTECH LIGO LABORATORY   Pasadena, CA
December 2004 - present

Postdoctoral scholar, currently Visitor in Physics
Gravitational-wave data analysis. Development and implementation of algorithms to search for unmodeled bursts of gravitational radiation in data from interferometric detectors. Application of burst algorithms to detector characterization. Member of the LIGO Scientific Collaboration (LSC). Co-chair of LSC glitch working group and member of the LSC Burst analysis Group. Member of the LIGO/Virgo joint data anal sis workin group.

7.4 How can I highlight how my work experience fits in with the post I am applying for? What key words should I try to insert?

Most companies and recruiters use applicant-tracking systems in order to scan CVs for key words. The key words that the systems are searching for will be the same key words that appear in the job description.

So if you are applying for a job which has been advertised, analyse the job description and decide what the key words are. Then try and insert these key words in the most natural way possible into your CV.

Basically, the more matches the system finds between the job description and your CV, the more likely your CV will be read by a real person.

7.5 How can I make my key words stand out, yet not be too obtrusive?

Let's imagine that you want to further your career in the field of web management. Your objective in your CV (and in your LinkedIn profile) is to fill your CV with keywords connected with web management, but without making it too obvious. Here is a good example of how to achieve that aim.

Notice how the candidate writes some of his key words with initial capital letters (e.g. Web Producer). This makes his key words stand out to the human reader (but obviously makes no difference if his CV is simply being scanned automatically).

Head of Digital: July 2029 – present

Marketing Media plc, 15-25 Newton Street, Manchester, UK, M1 1HL

Leading a team comprising a Web Producer, Web Developer and a Film Producer/ Editor, responsible for the planning, strategy and delivery of a careers advice and inspiration website.

- Developed e-communications strategy to grow the Creative Choices audience
- Successful negotiation with Google to sponsor a Google Adwords account
- Set and monitored quality, accuracy and style guidelines for web content
- Developed new digital tools and web services, from idea stage, through specification to delivery

Web Manager 2024 – 2029

XYZ Legal Consulting, 17 Whitley Road, Newcastle Upon Tyne, UK. NE98 1BA

Developed and maintained online content; responsible for:

- research, design and compilation of legal compliance information delivered online
- the style, accessibility and accuracy of all content on the web.

How many times do you think the word *web* appeared in the above extract? Three, four, five times? The candidate has quite subtly managed to include his key word seven times (including *website*) - to the human eye it won't be too intrusive, and at the same time a recruiter's software will be able to find multiple instances thus increasing the candidate's chances of having his CV selected.

7.6 I am a recent graduate. My CV looks rather empty. What can I do to fill it up?

If you are student and your CV looks a little empty, then you might also consider including a future experience that you have arranged for the very near future. The example is of a student from England who wrote his CV in May and was hoping to get a job as an English teacher in October of the same year:

VGB Volunteers **English Teacher** July - August Surin, Thailand	In order to obtain some teaching experience, I am going to undertake a volunteer placement with a charity in Surin, Thailand for a month. The charity offers free English lessons to tuk-tuk drivers and civil servants, for whom the expansion of their knowledge of English will enhance their employability greatly, given the importance of tourism in Thailand.

The important thing is to be honest. However, you are also trying to 'sell' yourself to recruiters, so you can make your work experience sound relevant and worthwhile by adding relevant details.

Below is an extract from the Work Experience section of a CV of a 23 year-old girl who went to London to learn English and gain some work experience. She worked as a sales assistant in several clothes shops, and each time she changed job she managed to secure a slightly better position and salary. In her CV she manages to make the most of what was in reality fairly routine work, but which nevertheless contributed to sound work experience. She also manages to highlight the various sales and communication skills that she acquired.

Note how she devotes more space to her most recent experience, which thus gives a sense of her 'career' progression.

October 2029 – present, Aubin & Wills, Selfridges, Oxford Street

Position: personal stylist. Main activities: styling and fitting service. Developed knowledge of vintage clothing and British textile manufacturers. Looking after customers; offering advice and styling according to customer needs and requests. Excellent customer service and advanced cashier operations (dealing with customer complaints, exchanges, refunds, cashing up). Participated in live music nights in store, magazine and bloggers' events for the company's product launches as a denim consultant.

March 2029 – October 2029, Nigel Hall Menswear, Selfridges, Oxford Street

Position: personal stylist. Main activities: styling and fitting service. Looked after customers, offering advice and styling according to customer needs and requests. Developed knowledge of formal wear and styling. Excellent personal target achievement and customer service.

7.6 I am a recent graduate. My CV looks rather empty. What can I do to fill it up? (cont.)

March 2028 – March 2029, London Levi's Flagship Store, Regent Street

Position: denim expert and fitting consultant. Main activities: knowledge regarding the history and the treatment of denim, vintage clothing and different kinds of styling. Sewing and customizing skills (alteration service). Took part in several visual merchandising projects in store.

7.7 Is it worth mentioning my teaching experience, even if it does not directly relate to the post I am applying for?

Yes, definitely. If you have taught some undergraduate classes, you will have learned some useful skills while in the classroom, for example how to:

- stand up in front of an audience and overcome your nerves
- explain difficult concepts in a simple way
- manage people
- prepare lessons and presentation slides
- work within specific time frames

These are all very useful and transferable skills that any employer either in industry or academia will appreciate.

Below are two examples. Note that in both cases impersonal forms have been used. However, the candidate could also have written: *I composed, I advised.* One advantage of the impersonal style is that it saves space.

Teaching Experience

MIT Department of Physics Cambridge, MA

September 2025 – December 2025

Teaching Assistant

Taught sophomore level course on Quantum Mechanics.

Advised Anna Southern on her MIT undergraduate Physics thesis. Anna developed and applied experiments for identifying ...

Teaching Experience

September 2025 – December 2025, Teaching Assistant, MIT Department of Physics Cambridge, MA

- Sophomore level course on Quantum Mechanics.
- Advice to MIT Physics undergraduate for thesis.

7.8 How should I describe internships and other research experiences?

When you describe what you did during your periods of work / research experience, ensure that what you write provides evidence that you have relevant experience for the job you are applying for.

Below are two examples of how to describe an internship, i.e. a period of supervised training at a research laboratory or in a company.

EXAMPLE 1

	Internships and summer schools
Apr - Dec 2024	Internship at the European Space Agency, Paris led by Dr Spock. My research was part of the standardization process of DVB-S2. I studied both theoretical and computer simulation of the carrier phase and frequency recovery schemes for DVB-S2 applications. The challenge was to explore low complex synchronization solutions for dealing with the high level of transmitter/receiver oscillator's phase noise. The outcome of this work was submitted for several ESA patent applications. I managed a small group of researchers for part of the internship.
Jun - Aug 2023	Summer school at NASA, Houston, Texas. I worked alongside several scientists and astronauts and was trained in the following areas:

In Example 1, the candidate uses personal forms and verbs: *my research, I studied* and *I worked*. On the other hand, in Example 2 below the candidate uses a series of nouns (*analysis, development, implementation*) with few verbs. Both these styles are typical, the second is less likely to lead to mistakes in grammar.

Research Experience	HITECH HYTO LABORATORY, KYOTO, JAPAN *2023 - present* **Postdoctoral scholar, currently Visitor in Physics** Gravitational-wave data analysis. Development and implementation of algorithms to search for unmodeled bursts of gravitational radiation in data from interferometric detectors. Member of the HYTO Scientific Collaboration (HSC). Co-chair of HSC glitch working group and member of the PHYTO analysis group. QTX CENTER FOR SPACE RESEARCH, OXFORD, UK *July 2022 - Jan 2023* **Sponsored Research Technical Staff** Design, construction, and operation of an experimental apparatus to measure correlated magnetic and seismic fluctuations between the two QTX observatory sites.

7.9   I have done some jobs that don't seem to fit under the heading Work Experience, can I call them 'Other Work Experience'?

Ideally, you don't want too many headings in your CV. So try and fit all your work experiences under one simple heading.

However, if you have little work experience and your CV looks rather empty, then you might want to fill it up with a new section. Here is an example:

OTHER WORK EXPERIENCE

Aug 2030: Research Internship at the New Policy Institute, London

- During this one month internship at a think-tank in London I helped to compile a major report about poverty and social exclusion within the UK. In particular I was investigating the effect of poverty and inequality on crime rates and health.

2028 –2030: teaching assistant, Altrincham Grammar School, UK

- I worked once a week at a grammar school in Cheshire with a group of five students aged 15-17. My role was to act as an informed and resourceful role model and to give the students a different perspective on their studies. This included helping the older students with career advice and university applications, and showing the younger students a range of options of higher education such as applying for college and apprenticeships.

- I worked both one-to-one and with groups of students and I taught them how to use various online resources which would help them with their studies.

Some jobs that you have done (or still do) may have nothing to do with your career path. You may have done them simply to earn money during the holidays or to support your expenses at university. Such jobs include babysitting, working in bars and shops, and doing voluntary work. They are worth mentioning because they indicate that you are:

- a responsible person (if some parents leave their child with you they must consider you to be responsible and mature)

- able to work with all kinds of people

- independent - you don't just rely on your parents to give you money

Rather than having a separate section, you can list these jobs under Personal Interests.

7.10 Work Experience: Do's and Don'ts

➤ Separate each experience.

➤ List as follows: i) date ii) company / organization iii) position iv) key roles played

➤ Dates: reverse chronological order.

➤ Grammar and conciseness: verbs without pronouns at beginning of sentences (e.g. *Developed* rather than *I developed*).

➤ Insert as many key words as is reasonably possible.

➤ Key words should be those in the advertisement for the job your are seeking, or on similar job specifications for people in your field if you are not applying for a specific job.

➤ Make your experience sound both relevant and dynamic.

➤ Only have a separate publications section if you are applying for a job in academia. Consider having this section as a separate document (i.e. not a direct part of your CV) or simply use a link to a webpage where your publications are listed.

Chapter 8
Technical and Soft Skills

Factoids

❖ Nearly one-third of US citizens feel that it is not too important or not important at all to speak a second language.

❖ The number of children and students studying languages in the UK has dropped considerably, and less money is being invested in language research. Apparently, this lack of language skills has led to a lack of interpreters and is making it harder for international anti-terrorism squads, for example, to work together.

❖ The CIA has a list of five languages it considers the most difficult to learn for native English speakers. Of the five languages in that group, Japanese is considered the most difficult. The other four languages are Arabic, Mandarin, Cantonese, and Korean.

❖ In 1918 (i.e. more than 100 years ago) data collected by the Carnegie Foundation found that technical skills (also known as hard skills) account for only 15% of future success at work, while 85% come from soft skills, i.e. ability to communicate well with other people and get on with them (likeability).

❖ Employers in the U.S. spend almost three quarters of their training budget on hard skills, despite the fact that soft skills are six times more important than hard skills.

❖ Research in the U.S. has shown that it is not a candidate's IQ, technical knowledge, socio-economic background or education that determine a successful career. Instead it is emotional intelligence i.e. interpersonal competence, building and managing positive personal relationships (e.g. earning trust and networking), self-awareness, and social awareness.

❖ Experts recommend NOT using the following expressions: *detail-oriented, flexible, independent, motivated, multi-tasker, strong work ethic, self-motivated.* Others recommend that you SHOULD use: *accurate, adaptable, confident, hard-working, innovative, pro-active, reliable, responsible.*

❖ The inhabitants of countries which broadcast movies and other TV programs directly in English (e.g., Scandinavian countries, Holland, Portugal) tend to speak and understand English much better than those countries where movies are dubbed (France, Germany, Italy).

© Springer Nature Switzerland AG 2019
A. Wallwork, *English for Academic CVs, Resumes, and Online Profiles*,
English for Academic Research, https://doi.org/10.1007/978-3-030-11090-1_8

8.1 What's the buzz?

A) Complete the table.

ADJECTIVE	KEY QUALITIES TO HAVE TO GET A JOB	YOU WOULD PUT IN YOUR CV AS AN ACCURATE DESCRIPTION OF YOURSELF	WOULD NOT LOOK POSITIVE ON A CV (YOURS OR ANYONE ELSE'S)
aggressive			
attractive			
competitive			
creative			
dependable			
generous			
hard working			
loyal			
objective			
patient			
proactive			
punctual			
sensitive			
uninhibited			

B) Imagine a new person is going to join your research team. What ten qualities would you want this person to have?

Look at the key for what over 1000 PhD students said they would rate as the top ten qualities in a potential colleague. Would you add any of these qualities to your own list?

This chapter details how to list your technical and language skills. You will discover the dangers of having a separate section entitled 'Communication Skills', and how to report such soft skills throughout the CV in a more indirect way.

8.2 How should I list my technical skills?

Look at the extract from a CV below. What impression do you have? What would be a good solution?

Software Skills	Good knowledge of Matlab / Simulink.
	Good knowledge of C/C++ language.
	Good knowledge of Java language.
	Good knowledge of Html/Javascript.
	Good knowledge of ASP.
	Good knowledge of PHP.
	Good knowledge of Visual Studio.
	Good knowledge of query language (MySql).
	Good knowledge of Unix operating systems (including Freebsd, Kubuntu and Debian).
	Good knowledge of Latex.
	Good knowledge of Doxygen.
	Intermediate knowledge of Labview.

There are many problems with the example above. The most obvious is the repetition of 'good knowledge'. It would be much more concise to do as follows:

Software Skills

I have good knowledge of the following: Matlab / Simulink; C/C++; Java; HTML/Javascript, ASP, PHP

Intermediate knowledge: Labview.

The other problem is credibility - is it possible to have 'good knowledge' of so many systems and languages? Just list the technical skills that are listed in the company's job specifications or which you think might in any case be useful for the job you are applying for.

To learn more about listing your technical skills see this page from Monster Worldwide Inc, a global employment website: https://www.monster.com/career-advice/article/show-your-skills-on-your-it-resume

8.3 Under what section should I put my language skills? And how do I mention them?

You can either have Language Skills as a separate section. Or you can have a section entitled Skills under which you put your language skills and technical skills.

If you are applying for a position in Europe, you can use the levels from the Common European Framework of Reference (CEFR) for Languages. The levels of language proficiency are classified from A1 (basic) to C2 (fluent) see: http://en.wikipedia.org/wiki/Common_European_Framework_of_Reference_for_Languages

Given that the Europass format takes up a lot of space You could simply write:

Korean: mother tongue; **Chinese**: C2; **English**: spoken B2, listening B2, written and reading C1

Another alternative:

Korean: mother tongue; **Chinese**: fluent; **English**: TOEFL (101/120)

In the above example, TOEFL is an exam (www.ets.org/toefl) which has a score out of 120. Other typical exams are IELTS (takeielts.britishcouncil.org/find-out-about-results/understand-your-ielts-scores)

and the Cambridge exams (www.cambridgeenglish.org/exams-and-qualifications/).

If you are very short of space, you can list the languages you know in your Personal Details section. For example:

Kamran Kamatchi

914 West 10th Street, Hazleton, PA, 18209, USA

k.kamatchi@gmail.com (+11) 7525 446779

Languages: English (native), Bengali (native), Spanish (good working knowledge)

Note that in the US, the Interagency Language Roundtable (ILR) scale is used. Below are the equivalents.

CEFR	ILR	CEFR	ILR	CEFR	ILR
A1	0/0+	B1	1+	C1	3/3+
A2	1	B2	2/2+	C2	4/4

8.4 Should I have a separate section entitled 'Communication Skills'?

Look at the section below from a CV? Would it apply to you?

Communications skills

My experience has enabled me to build relationships easily and solve problems fast and efficiently. I can work under pressure both in a team and independently. Responsibility, punctuality and efficiency have always formed part of my work.

The above qualities could apply to anyone, not just to one person in particular.

Your CV should clearly demonstrate that you have these skills without you stating this explicitly.

You may have acquired many communication skills and not necessarily directly during research or employment. In any case such skills will probably be useful for the position you are seeking. However these skills should be implicit in the Education, Work Experience (see end of this subsection) and Personal Interests sections of your CV as well as in the cover letter and reference letters. They should not be listed in a separate section.

Below is an extract from a section entitled 'Personal Skills and Competences'. What would the HR person learn from the information given? Basically, that this candidate is the same as every other candidate. The problem is that lists of such skills are completely pointless unless substantiated by evidence.

Social skills and competences	Ability to build relationships easily I solve problems easily and efficiently.
	Team player
Organisational skills and competences	Experience in organizing groups of students
Other skills and competences	Ability to work under pressure

8.4 Should I have a separate section entitled 'Communication Skills'? (cont.)

Below is an example of how to integrate some of your soft skills into the body of your CV, in this case the Work Experience section. For the purposes of this book, the soft skills are highlighted in italics.

Jul 2027 – Sep 2028: Fermilab – Fermi National Accelerator Laboratory, Batavia, IL, USA

Worked as a Computer Engineer at Fermilab in the Accelerator Division under the supervision of Brian Chase and Paul Joiremann. *Headed up various small internal work groups.*

Fermilab conducts basic research into particle physics. *Part of my duties included technical presentations of Fermilab research projects to interested partners.*

Development of hardware-software interfaces and client-server interfaces using C/C++, DOOCS, Labview. *This included solving critical problems in very short timeframes relating to high-energy physics.*

Note how the candidate has not stated explicitly that she has certain soft skills, but has alluded to them indirectly. The first paragraph highlights the candidate's team working skills, the second her presentation skills, and the third her problem-solving skills and her ability to work to tight deadlines. Clearly, it is not necessary to write about your soft skills for every work or educational experience you have had, just four or five examples highlighting different skills should be sufficient. You can emphasize these skills again in your cover letter.

8.5 How should I talk about my personality and soft skills?

HR want to know not just about your technical skills and experience but also need concrete evidence of these skills. They also want evidence that you have good communication skills e.g. an ability to work in teams, and to do presentations.

Would you write the following?

> *I hate human relationships. I'm lazy, with a zero capacity for teamwork. I have rarely worked during my studies and I never meet deadlines. It is important for me never to finish my projects.*

You wouldn't; so don't write this either:

> *I love human relationships. I'm proactive with a high capacity for teamwork. I work hard. I like to complete my projects and goals.*

Firstly, the qualities mentioned are obvious. Anyone hoping to get a decent job should have such qualities. Secondly, the candidate has provided no evidence that he/she actually has such qualities.

Instead you need to write something that is specific to you and that really demonstrates these qualities.

Companies are interested in various soft skills, for which you need to provide evidence.

Below are various examples that you could write in your cover letter.

ABILITY TO WORK IN A TEAM

> I have worked in several research teams and also during an internship at IBM in Houston in 2020.

PROFESSIONALISM, PRO-ACTIVE, FLEXIBILITY, MEETING DEADLINES

> During my internship I worked on several very diverse projects and managed to meet all the deadlines.

PROBLEM SOLVING SKILLS

> The two projects I worked on involved solving complex engineering problems and I very much enjoyed taking part in brain-storming sessions with the team.

PRESENTATION SKILLS

> I presented two of the three projects I worked on to clients, both of whom then went ahead and purchased the product.

ABILITY TO WRITE TECHNICAL DOCUMENTS

> My duties include liaising with clients and writing specifications.

8.5 How should I talk about my personality and soft skills? (cont.)

Obviously you don't need to mention all of the points above. You need to judge which ones would be the most relevant for the job and which ones you have practical experience of that you can demonstrate in your letter.

When mentioning soft skills, it is essential that you substantiate these skills. In the example below the candidate actually proves that he does not have the skill that he claims to have (i.e. good English).

> *Even if* I'm *not expert* in all programming languages *your* request, I am highly motivated to learn new skills and have a good attitude to relate with customers and to find solutions to complex problems.
>
> Additionally I *have good knowledge of english language*, I'm *spanish mother tongue* and I live in Quito.

The example above is full of English mistakes: *even if* (even though), *not expert* (not an expert), *your request* (you request), *good knowledge of english language* (a good knowledge of English), *spanish mother tongue* (my native language is Spanish). Clearly, not only is the candidate's English poor (rather than good), but he also hasn't even bothered to check his letter. This creates a very bad impression, and his CV is likely to be quickly discarded.

8.6　How should I outline my skills in a resume?

You can include a skills section either before or after your Education section. Given that a resume is generally a one-page document, you will have very little space. Keep it to 2-3 lines by writing as follows:

Skills

Languages: Spanish (native speaker), English (TOEFL). Computer: Microsoft Word, Excel, Powerpoint. Technical: excellent knowledge of QXC calibrators, good knowledge of UYT.

Before being admitted into many US universities to do business / management courses, you may be requested to carry out a GMAT - a graduate management admission test. This test assesses your analytical, writing, verbal and reading skills in English. Go on Wikipedia to learn more.

8.7　Skills: Do's and Don'ts

➢ Do not have a separate section for communication skills. Just have sections for technical skills and language skills

➢ Integrate your communication / soft skills into the other sections of your CV and into your cover letter.

➢ Use the most concise format possible, unless you have space that you wish to fill.

➢ Do not exaggerate your skills and experience. You cannot be an 'expert' or have 'good knowledge' of everything.

➢ Do not mention languages for which you only have a basic knowledge, unless the job specification specifically states that some knowledge of that language would be 'useful'

➢ Do not exaggerate your language level If you claim that you have an 'advanced' knowledge of English but there are mistakes in the English of your CV and cover letter, then you will immediately lose credibility. Also, if all or part of the interview is conducted in English (either over the phone or face to face) and you fail to perform to an advanced level, the interviewer may suspect that you may have exaggerated other parts of your CV too.

➢ If you are not sure of your level, then get a qualified EFL / ESL teacher (English as a Foreign Language / English as a Second Language) to give you a quick test.

Chapter 9
Personal Interests

Factoids

❖ According to Business Insider there are 13 hobbies that candidates should consider including in their resume: yoga, extreme adventure sports, video production, endurance sports, captain of a team sport, blogging, mountain climbing, paying an instrument, volunteering, photography, gardening, fantasy football, and anything unusual (in a good way).

❖ Although some may view including a section on hobbies as being irrelevant or unprofessional, many experts agree that talking about personal interests is one way to make a candidate stand out from the competition.

❖ A personal interests section may help a potential employer understand the candidate better as a person, rather than just a list of qualifications and experiences.

❖ Students at the University of York in England drink more alcohol than any other university in the UK - the equivalent of nearly five liters of lager per week.

❖ In the US, the average college student attends 62 parties per year.

❖ Brigham Young University in Provo (Utah, USA) holds the record for being the US university where you are most likely to meet your future spouse.

❖ Undergraduates in the USA often form fraternities and sororities, which are single-sex organizations for male and female students, respectively. The names of these groups are often taken from Greek letters (alpha, beta etc) and their members are sometimes known as 'Greeks'.

❖ The University of Cambridge in England has over 400 registered clubs and societies for students.

❖ Estonia holds the record for the highest proportion of female graduates - more than two thirds are women.

© Springer Nature Switzerland AG 2019

A. Wallwork, *English for Academic CVs, Resumes, and Online Profiles*,
English for Academic Research, https://doi.org/10.1007/978-3-030-11090-1_9

9.1 What's the buzz?

A) Assuming that you include a Personal Interests section in your CV, discuss what interests you have outside work and if these interests could be mentioned on your CV. Think about what these interests reveal about you and how they might relate to your approach to work and study.

B) Look at the first factoid on the previous page. Why do think those particular hobbies are recommended? (To find the answer see: https://it.businessinsider.com/hobbies-look-great-on-resume-2017-2/?r=US&IR=T)

Now discuss which of these hobbies and interests would you put on your CV and LinkedIn?

- Reading
- Sports
- Traveling
- Playing the guitar
- Salsa dancing
- Sailing
- Computer games
- Voluntary work
- Opera music
- Baby sitting
- Politics (member of x party)

This chapter discusses which of your hobbies and interests you should (and should not) mention in your CV and your online profiles. You will learn how to use your interests to provide evidence of your soft skills. Non-work-related sections (e.g. awards, volunteering) in LinkedIn are also briefly discussed here.

9.2 Under what heading should I put my hobbies and interests?

You can use one of the following depending on the type of information you plan to give in this section.

- Hobbies and Interests
- Personal Interests
- Extra-curricular Activities

9.3 Which, if any, of my hobbies and interests should I mention in my CV and my online profiles?

The following quotation comes from the website of REED, which is an employment agency based in the UK. Discuss to what extent you agree with the quotation and also whether you think it is a good idea to include a Personal Interests section in your CV.

You've got no idea how the person reviewing your application will react to your hobbies, so it's best to leave them off unless they're relevant to the role. No hobbies at all is better than 'socializing with friends'.

Your interests and what you do outside of your academic life are important because they give an idea of your personality. They are unique and give HR people and recruiters into your character that are difficult to demonstrate in the rest of the CV.

On LinkedIn your interests serve to give readers (not just fellow academics but also recruiters) a bigger picture of who you are and what you might be like to work with.

Consider including activities that:

- show you have a social conscience (e.g. voluntary / charity work)
- highlight your leadership skills (e.g. team captain of a sports team, sports trainer)
- demonstrate your communication skills
- are fun and have positive connotations (e.g. salsa dancing, playing the saxophone), or interesting (e.g. acting), or creative (e.g. pottery, short story writing)
- indicate that others consider you to be a responsible person (e.g. babysitting)
- unusual without being strange (e.g. falconry, acrobatics)

9.4 What hobbies and interests should I avoid mentioning?

Avoid mentioning things that most people probably do (e.g. *reading, traveling*). Instead, be specific. Rather than *sports*, write say *swimming, hockey* etc. If you put *traveling*, maybe say your favorite destinations.

Do not put activities that are political, religious, or contentious (e.g. *hunting, shooting*).

HR people are interested in your ability to work in a team and in your social skills. So, avoid solitary or nerdy activities (e.g. *computer games, collecting stamps*).

Some activities that most people would consider to be very positive and altruistic, such as being a blood donor, may by a company be considered negatively. In the case of donating blood, for example, this may involves having to take time off work for which the company may have to pay you. Paying you for not being at work doesn't usually make companies happy!

Finally, avoid anything that people tend have strong opinions about. For example, people tend to either love or hate board games or role playing games. So these are best avoided.

9.5 How can I use my interests to provide evidence of my soft skills?

Below is what a PhD student in Cognitive Sciences wrote under 'Hobbies and Interests'.

> I love traveling because I enjoy meeting new people and staying in different socio-cultural environments. My interest in foreign languages and cultures has increased my metalinguistic skills in living and working with people from different cultures thus I have no problems to integrate myself socially. I have been doing various kinds of sports (dance, horse-riding, kung fu, capoeira angola) since I was 5 years old. These activities have played an important role in forming my sense of duty and organization and mostly my interest towards new and different cultures and persons.

She has used her interest in traveling, languages and sport to show her social skills and the fact she is interested in a wide variety of activities and thus has a broad skills base. She has exploited this section to give the reader a clearer idea of who she is as a person, and what makes her stand out from the other candidates.

9.6   Should I write a list or a short paragraph?

The candidate in the previous subsection opted for a paragraph and used around 100 words but clearly believed that such information would help her chances of being hired. Obviously, if your CV is very full, you would not have the space to include such information.

So she could have listed her interests as follows:

> traveling, living and working in foreign countries, sports (dance, horse-riding, kung fu, capoeira angola)

The advantages of a list are that it:

- takes up much less space
- is quicker to read

However a paragraph, if you have space, can give the HR person a much clearer picture of who you are.

9.7 What are the dangers of writing a paragraph?

Here is example from a young graduate (a native English speaker) who was looking for a job in teaching.

> I like to spend my free time outside, playing rugby or walking, working in the garden or reading. I've played for the Altrincham rugby team for several years and worked along-side the youth team. I was involved in the founding of the Rugby Society of Reading University. I regularly listen to live music whenever I have the opportunity and enjoy playing the guitar. I have a keen interest in travel, and spent seven months after completing my academic studies fulfilling my dream of travelling the world. I visited China, Singapore, Australia, New Zealand and the United States of America during my trip. I feel this trip opened me up to experiences and empathy which would be unattainable in Britain and as such have made me a better rounded person. While away on my travels I spent time working on farms in New Zealand; I found this work gave me good perspective on all the types of work in the world. In my life I have spend a lot of time working in groups or teams, my personality is well suited to the group environment. Groups I have been involved with have helped organise holidays for the disabled, music festivals for charity as well my personal achievements of climbing Mt. Kilimanjaro and working in Tanzanian School.

The problem with writing so much is that you:

- have to use complete grammatical sentences, and thus probably make more mistakes (even this native speaker makes a mistake: *I have spend* rather than *I have spent*)
- may be prone to waffle (i.e. not be very precise or concise)
- use up a lot of space

You also need to ensure that this section is organized clearly, just as in the other sections.

By writing so much, you are assuming that the hirer has the time to read all that you have written. However, it may depend on who the hirer is. If you are looking for a job for a small organization, and the job requires a candidate with an interesting personality and with good communication, then the hirer may be truly interested in reading about all your personal activities.

9.7 What are the dangers of writing a paragraph? (cont.)

So, again a list might be a better option. Below is an example of how the above candidate could have listed his interests. Note how it is divided into mini sections, which gives the idea of an organized mind and who also wishes to communicate information in the clearest and simplest way possible.

Sports and outdoor activities: rugby (I play for my local team, and founded a rugby society at university), walking, gardening.

Traveling: I have visited China, Singapore, Australia, New Zealand and the United States of America, Tanzania (where I climbed Mt. Kilimanjaro)

Volunteer work: organizing holidays for the disabled, music festivals to raise money for charity (I also play the guitar).

By writing a list you will make less mistakes. You can also provide interesting details about yourself that provide evidence of your soft skills, e.g. the parts in brackets in the list above.

9.8 Are there any other tricks for gaining the hirer's attention through my Personal Interests section?

There are two simple tricks you can use:

Firstly, read the job specification carefully and see if there are any non-technical requirements that you could somehow insert into your Personal Interests section.

Below are three extracts from a job specification as a patent examiner.

```
The job of a European patent examiner demands a unique
combination of scientific expertise, analytical thinking,
language skills and an interest in intellectual property law.

You should have a genuine interest in technology, an eye for
detail and an analytical mind.

Applicants must also be willing to relocate to Munich, The Hague
or Berlin
```

Through your interests you could try to provide evidence that you have the skills required. For example, someone who paints or has reviewed papers will have *an eye for detail*, someone who has traveled frequently and who has preferably been to Germany or the Netherlands shows that they wouldn't have a problem to *relocate* and will probably have *language skills*, and someone who designs and makes their own model planes probably has *a genuine interest in technology, an eye for detail and an analytical mind.*

Secondly, if you know exactly who is going to read your CV, then you can find out this person's personal interests on LinkedIn, Facebook, or on their blog or personal website. If you find any genuine matches between your interests and their interests, then you can mention them. But at the interview do not mention that you looked at your interviewer's web pages!

For more very useful information on writing a Personal Interests section see:

https://www.resumecoach.com/write-a-resume/personal-interests/#should-you-include-your-hobbies-on-a-resume

https://www.myfuturerole.com/article/hobbies-and-interests/

9.9 How should I talk about my interests on LinkedIn?

You can talk about your interests in the same way as on a CV. To get some ideas for what to include and what not, look on the profiles of your connections and see how they list their interests.

I believe that you should not design this section to attract recruiters or potential clients.

9.10 I don't have any Honors & Awards. Is it a problem?

No. You do not need to complete this section.

9.11 What about Volunteer Experience and Causes?

It is safe to talk about volunteer experiences as they imply that you will have learned various social skills. However, listing the causes you support is potentially danger-ous - what if the HR person shares very different political views from you?

Even though LinkedIn constantly encourages you to 'complete' your profile, you might consider simply leaving this section blank.

9.12 Personal Interests: Do's and Don'ts

➢ Ensure you have a Personal Interests section - this enables interested HR people to get a clearer picture of you as a person. In any case, the uninterested HR person can ignore this section if they wish.

➢ Do not mention activities and interests that may have a negative connotation for some people.

➢ Only use a paragraph if you have excess space. Otherwise use a list, preferably divided into three or four mini subsections.

➢ Exploit your interests to highlight your soft skills and the skills requested in the job specification.

Chapter 10
References and Reference Letters

Double meanings in reference letters

❖ A man like him is hard to find.

❖ All in all, I cannot say enough good things about this candidate or recommend her too highly.

❖ She could not care less about the number of hours she has to put in.

❖ You would indeed be fortunate to get this person to work for you.

❖ I most enthusiastically recommend this candidate with no qualifications whatsoever.

❖ I would urge you to waste no time in making this candidate an offer of employment.

❖ There is nothing you can teach a man like him.

❖ She's an unbelievable worker.

❖ I can assure you that no person would be better for the job.

❖ Every hour with him was a happy hour.

© Springer Nature Switzerland AG 2019
A. Wallwork, *English for Academic CVs, Resumes, and Online Profiles*,
English for Academic Research, https://doi.org/10.1007/978-3-030-11090-1_10

10.1 What's the buzz?

A) Look back at the previous page and match 'recommendations' with the real meanings below.

e.g. *A man like him is hard to find* = this employee is always absent.

1. Better to employ no one rather than give this person a job.

2. Dishonest.

3. Drunk at work.

4. Exceptionally lazy.

5. No diplomas.

6. Not worth employing.

7. Not worth employing.

8. Rarely at work.

9. Unbelievably unintelligent.

B) Analyse the reference letter below for a graduate, written by her professor.

- Find at least three points why this letter is likely to make a positive impression on the reader.

- How is the letter structured? What is the purpose of each paragraph?

Adele Tulloch

PARAGRAPH 1 I am a Professor of Information Engineering at the University of Manchester and I have great pleasure in writing a reference for Adele Tulloch. I first came into contact with Adele when she attended two courses in Computer Networking that I give to Master's students in Computer Engineering - her scores in the examinations were excellent, i.e. way above the average.

PARAGRAPH 2 After completing her Master's, Adele won a 5-month research scholarship targeted at the bandwidth estimation of the bottleneck link along an Internet path.

PARAGRAPH 3 During this time Adele worked in my research group. Adele showed no difficulty in absorbing new knowledge and in gaining the needed knowhow. She was both proactive and creative, often producing truly original and outstanding results (see attached list of papers).

10.1 What's the buzz? (cont.)

PARAGRAPH 4 Adele not only has excellent technical skills (x, y, z), but has several other qualities that I find to be quite rare in someone of her age. Her high level of independence meant she was able to carry out the work by herself with only occasional guidance from me. I found her very receptive and easy to talk to. She had a useful knack of being able to take my ideas to the next possible level and suggest possible directions of further investigations. She always managed to meet any deadlines I set her and always with a self-critical eye on her own work.

PARAGRAPH 5 In summary, I have absolutely no hesitation in recommending Adele Tulloch as a xxxx. Please feel free to contact me should you need any further details.

Best regards

Prof. Jo O'Donnell

Referees and reference letters can make a big difference to your chances of getting an interview and thus a job. This chapter explains how to choose your referees and how to write a reference letter (including the option of writing it yourself and getting the referee to sign it). It is not recommended to have a glowingly positive reference letter, but to include also possible areas where you need to improve your skills.

10.2   Do I need to provide the names of referees on my CV?

In the context of a CV, a referee is someone you have worked for or collaborated with, and who can provide an objective appraisal of your technical and social skills.

In most Anglo countries it is customary to provide the names of referees. This enables potential employers to contact your referees to:

- check that you are who you say you are, and that you have done what you say you have done
- learn more about your personality and skills

HR use references as part of the screening process of candidates.

So, yes, you do need to provide references.

10.3   Where should I put my referees on my CV?

At the end of your CV have a separate section entitled 'References' in which you list three or four people. Provide the following information:

- name

- their relationship to you

- where they work

- their email address (so that the HR person can contact them)

- their website (so that HR can learn more about them)

For example:

> Professor Pinco Pallino (my thesis tutor), University of London, p.pallino@londonuni.ac.uk, www.pincopallino.com

> Professor Zack Madman (in whose lab I did a 3-month internship), University of Harvard, z.madman@harvard.edu, www.harvard.edu/madman

You do not need to write any more than above. For example, the referee's postal address and telephone number are redundant, as it is highly likely that first contact will be via email. The other problem with providing more information is that it can take up a lot of space as highlighted in the examples below. If you provided five references using this format, it would occupy 15 lines - far too much space.

Clare Krumpet (CELTA Tutor): Liverpool Academy of English, St Margaret's Chambers, 5 Newton Street, Liverpool, UK, L1 1HL. Tel – +44 (0)161 - 237 5619 Email c.krumpet@livacenglish

Jo Bloggs (Self Help Services Volunteer Coordinator): Self Help Services, Zion Community Resource, 339 Stretford Road, Hulme, Liverpool, UK, L15 ZEE. Tel – +44 (0)844 477 9971 Email – j.bloggs@selfhelpservices.org.uk

10.4 Will HR people and recruiters contact my referees?

It depends on where in the world they are located. Many HR people and recruiters in the USA and UK and other Anglo countries will contact your referees typically via email but also via phone. A typical email they might write to your referee is:

> Re Brandy Dalgarno
>
> The above named student has applied to our Department for admission to a Postgraduate Programme of Study (PhD) and has given your name as someone who can inform me of her ability to undertake advanced study and research leading to a higher degree in Physics.
>
> Would you please let me know, in confidence, your opinion of Mr Wallwork's ability, character and capacity for postgraduate study.
>
> Thank you in advance for your cooperation.

10.5 What is a reference letter? How important is it?

A 'reference' is a letter written by a referee, i.e. the person you worked for or collaborated with - typically your professor / tutor and people you have worked for/ with during an internship. Or if you have work experience, then the letter could be written by a past employer.

In this letter the referee gives a brief summary of your technical skills and also your personality (how motivated you are, how easy you are to work with, how proactive you are etc).

It is extremely important.

You create your CV and cover letter, so the picture that you present of yourself is naturally very subjective. Also, when you describe your soft skills, you are describing these skills from your own point of view and it is very difficult for you to prove within the CV and cover letter that you really have these skills.

A reference letter is written by a third party who generally has no vested interest in you getting a particular job or not. The role of this third party is to present an objective view of you and your personality.

For the HR person, a reference letter is a kind of guarantee that you are who you say you are.

10.6   Who should I ask to write my reference letter? Can I write it myself?

Whenever you work / collaborate with someone in a lab or a company, get a written reference from someone there. You can then use these references as and when you need them. Also, get permission from these people to put their names, position and email addresses on your CV.

Many of the people you ask for a reference might appreciate it if you write the letter yourself and then submit it to them for their signature and approval. This saves the referee a lot of time.

Writing the letter yourself has several advantages. You can decide:

- the exact content
- the structure
- the length
- what to emphasize and what not to mention

But remember, if you write the letter yourself, you must submit it to the relevant person for their approval and signature.

In some cases, your reference person may be contacted directly by the company or institute where you have applied for a position and the employer may send a form to fill out. It makes sense for you to fill out the form with your professor, or at least to request that you be able to see the form before it is sent back to the employer. If you can, get hold of such forms in advance, and plan carefully how to answer the questions.

10.7 How should I ask someone to write a reference letter for me?

Ideally you should ask the person while you are still working for him / her. Then they will have time to prepare the letter before you leave. You can say to this person:

> *I was wondering if it would be possible for you to write me a reference letter.*

If you decide you would prefer to write the letter yourself, then you can add:

> *If you like, I can write the letter myself and then submit it to you for approval.*

If you are not dealing with your referee face to face but via email, you can write:

> *Dear Professor Smith*
>
> *First of all I just wanted to say how useful I found the three months in your laboratory. It was particularly useful because ...*
>
> *I was wondering if it would be possible for you to write me a reference letter.*
>
> *I am applying for a position at ... / I am applying for a job as a ... at ... It would be much appreciated if you could write the letter by the end of next week.*
>
> *Alternatively, for your convenience, I could write the letter myself and then submit it to you for your approval and signature.*
>
> *Best wishes*

The structure of the above email is:

1. mention the time spent at the referee's department, institute, company etc

2. add some details of the usefulness of the time spent there

3. ask for a reference letter

4. say why you need the letter, i.e. the position you are applying for

5. give a deadline for the receipt of the letter

6. suggest that you write it yourself

10.8 How important is it for the reference letter to be written in good English?

Very.

A reference letter that is full of mistakes, even if it was not written by you, may undermine what it says about you.

If you write your own letter (10.6) then you can also have the letter checked by a native English speaker to make sure there are no grammatical mistakes. Remember that the level of English of the person who you ask to be your referee may not be very good.

In any case, even if your referee writes your letter, you can still have it checked by a professional. You can then resubmit it to your referee for them to sign again. You may find such a procedure embarrassing but you can write an email such as:

> *Dear* name of referee
>
> *Thank you so much for writing me the reference letter, I very much appreciate it.*
>
> *A native English speaking friend of mine happened to read it and noticed a couple of mistakes.*
>
> *Attached is a revised version. Would you mind signing it again for me.*
>
> *Thank you for your help.*
>
> *Best regards*

10.9 Example of a poorly written letter

Below are the first two paragraphs of a letter written for a student, Melanie Guyot, by her university professor. As you read the first sentence, try to understand who *teacher* refers to - Melanie or her professor? What other mistakes can you find?

Letter in support to the candidacy of Melanie Guyot both as XXX at the XXX

I am writing this, having assessed the capacity of Melanie Guyot both as a teacher of Medical Robotics (Master of Science in Biomedical Engineering at the University of XX) and during her work as a majoring in biomedical engineering at the Biorobotics Institute, Creative Design area of which I am the coordinator. Also in this last year I got to know the skills and potential of the candidate as a research fellow at our institute.

During the master thesis, I could appreciate its intuitiveness in solving real physical problems that helped to efficiently design an hydraulic actuation system for minimally invasive surgical instruments. She has been able, in that context, to greatly expand her knowledge, showing excellent ability to work in multidisciplinary field of research.

The first sentence contains 52 words in a long series of subclauses. It is very poorly structured and includes ambiguity (who is the *teacher*?). In the second paragraph there are numerous mistakes in the English:

during the master thesis = during her Master's

its intuitiveness = her intuitiveness

an hydraulic = a hydraulic

she has been able = she was able

work in multidisciplinary field = work in a multidisciplinary field

The result is that the referee's poorly written letter reflects badly on the candidate. The reader (HR; recruiter) might associate the referees' poor English and structure with unreliability and lack of professionalism. This lack of professionalism might then, unfortunately, be transferred to the candidate as well. To see

10.10 How should I structure my reference letter?

Your reference letter needs a very clear structure which will highlight your key skills (both technical and soft) and will thus act as an objective support to what you have written in your CV. Here is a possible structure:

0) Heading

1) Positive opening sentence

2) Referee's position

3) Referee's connection to candidate

4) Details about candidate's qualifications

5) Reference to candidate's wonderful personality

6) Positive conclusion

7) Salutation

Now let's look at how the poorly written letter in 10.9 could be rewritten. Each paragraph of the letter is an example of the structure above.

Melanie Guyot [0]

It is a pleasure for me to have the opportunity to thoroughly recommend Melanie Guyot [for the position of ...] [1]

I am the coordinator of the Biorobotics Institute at the University of Monpellier. [2]

I was Melanie's supervisor while she was doing her Master's of Science in ... She was also a student in my class on medical robotics. [3]

During her Master's thesis, Melanie demonstrated great intuitiveness in solving ... In fact, she played a major role in ... She also ... [4]

Melanie has a bright and lively personality and works extremely well in teams, both as a team member and team leader. She showed a clear demonstration of these skills when ... [5]

I very much hope that her application will be taken into serious consideration as I am sure that Melanie Guyot represents an excellent candidate. [6]

Best regards [7]

Pierre Lepoof

(pierre.lepoof@institute.com)

10.10 How should I structure my reference letter? (cont.)

The letter above highlights the following points.

- There is no initial salutation, i.e. the letter is not addressed to anyone in particular. In fact, the letter is intended for anyone that Melanie chooses to write to.

- The heading of the letter simply contains the candidate's name, rather than adding the position that candidate is looking for on one specific occasion. This means that you can use the same reference letter for more than one job application.

- Each paragraph has a specific purpose. Also, by dividing the letter up into multiple paragraphs (rather than one or two long paragraphs), the reader will be able to quickly locate the information he/she is interested in.

- In Paragraph 2, the referee first establishes his / her credibility. The HR person needs to know that the reference is written by someone who is qualified to write such a letter. Then in Paragraph 3, the referee answers an HR person's question: How does the referee know the candidate?

- Paragraph 4 will probably be the longest paragraph in the letter, and may even be divided up into more than one paragraph. This is the part of the letter where the referee tries to establish the credibility of the candidate, and gives objective support to what the candidate has written in his/her CV. Further support is provided in Paragraph 5, which outlines the candidate's social / soft skills.

- When writing any kind of letter or email, it is good practice to begin and end on a positive note (Paragraphs 1 and 6).

- The final salutation is brief (*Best regards*). There is no need to write 'Feel free to contact me should you need further details'. The whole point of a reference letter is that the referee implicitly gives their permission to be contacted, so there is no need to state this. The aim is to keep the letter as concise as possible.

- The referee provides their email address (if this is not already on the header / footer of the letter) so that they can be contacted.

10.11 Is it acceptable and ethical for me to write my own reference letters? What are the dangers?

It is both acceptable and ethical to write your own reference letter, providing that your referee:

- sees the letter and approves the content
- checks that his / her contact details are correctly written on the letter
- signs the letter

But be aware of the dangers. Look at the beginnings of these letters. What do you notice about them?

Shanghai, December 3rd, 2027

To whom it may concern,

It is a pleasure to write this letter of reference for Dr. Fu Hao.

From December 2026 to July 2027 Ms. Fu Hao did her research work for her bachelor thesis in my group, supervised by Associate Prof. Zhaobin Yang. Due to her interests on "molecular design", she was working on ...

Shanghai, January 16th, 2028

To whom it may concern

It is a pleasure for me to write the reference letter of Dr. Fu Hao for her application of postdoc position.

In March 2027 Ms. Fu Hao started her PhD study in the field of Chemistry and Physics of Polymers at Shanghai Jiao Tong University (SJTU), China, under my supervision.

Bogota, December 3rd, 2029

To whom it may concern,

I am pleased to write this letter of recommendation for Dr. Fu Hao.

I met Fu Hao in 2027, during a Conference in Shanghai where she attended a session in which I was a speaker. After that she contacted me asking to join temporarily my research group during her last years of graduate studies pursuing a PhD degree in Chemistry at Shanghai Jiao Tong University.

She joined my research group at the end of 2028 ...

10.11   Is it acceptable and ethical for me to write my own reference letters? What are the dangers? (cont.)

The problem is that they all look the same both in terms of layout and content:

- the date is expressed using the same format
- the location of where the letter was written is always indicated (though this is not a recognized standard in Anglo countries)
- they all begin with *To whom it may concern*
- the opening sentence is very similar
- the name of the candidate is referred to in the same way - the first time as Dr and the second time as Ms

This may make the HR person suspect that the candidate has written her own reference letters, and that the referees themselves may actually have not seen the letters. So if you do write your own letter then try to use a slightly different format. You can modify the:

- date e.g. 10 March 2020; March 10th, 2020; March 10, 2020
- layout
- font
- use and non-use of paragraph indentation
- order that information is given
- salutations
- overall length of the letter

10.12 Is it OK for the reference letter to include negative information?

Yes. You need to be honest. And it also makes you sound more credible.

In the example below, the possibly negative information is highlighted in italics. Note that although this info might initially be interpreted as negative, a logical explanation is given.

> Once in Bogota she readily accepted to take up a new research topic (fluorinated latex blends for nanostructured coatings) that had been in stand by because of lack of specific financing, *only vaguely related to her previous research* but well within her already broad expertise and skills. In the following three years she actually did all the research work and achieved the results that allowed her to obtain her PhD from Jiao Tong University at the beginning of 2020.

> In the meanwhile, I had her work also on other projects that *did not allow her to write papers* due to confidentiality, but allowed me to finance her stay in Bogota after an initial period in which she had been supported by her University. These are the main reasons for the apparently long time it took her to complete her PhD and for the limited number of papers published.

> *Unfortunately I could not extend her contract* because of lack of adequate financing, but I am confident that with her good background, skills and expertise she will very quickly find a new postdoctoral position within an excellent research group.

The example above highlights how a cover letter can be used to explain any apparent anomalies in the CV, such as why you:

- apparently changed the course of your career (i.e. a seemingly illogical sequence of jobs or research positions)
- failed to publish the expected number of papers
- had to interrupt a particular internship

The same letter also contained these two comments:

> Her approach to scientific problems and to the interpretation of the experimental results is *still a little too focused on details*, however she is making great efforts to look at the broader picture.

> ....

> She is effective in reporting her results, *though she still requires some support* in the initial and final stages of writing a paper. For the latter issue, I believe I was not the best possible supervisor because I tend to always cover the final stage myself.

Having such negative information (which in this case is not too serious) makes you seem like a normal human being. Having a letter that is 100% praise may sound less credible - does this candidate really have no faults? do I want such a perfect person on my team?

10.13 Are there significant differences in style between the ways US and UK academics write reference letters?

Jonathan Birch is an Associate Professor in the Department of Philosophy, Logic and Scientific Method at the London School of Economics and Political Science and like all professors has to write reference letters for his students. Below is an extract from a <u>humorous</u> post from his Facebook page, which is reproduced with the kind permission of Jonathan Birch.

Academic letters of recommendation: a guide for the perplexed.

The American style:
"I have never recommended anyone more highly than this. Jones is, without doubt, the most agile thinker of his generation, and perhaps of any generation in living memory. I would like to say he will revolutionize the field, but such an understatement would do no justice to his true abilities. More likely, he will define an entirely new field, Jones Studies, that will enjoy such prestige that a Nobel Prize in Jones Studies will soon be created, with Jones as its inaugural recipient. Indeed, I would not be surprised to see Jones win three or four Nobel prizes, given his strong side-interests in medicine, physics and peace. While you may be concerned that Jones has no publications, I assure you this is only because Jones's research, like Darwin's, is so potent that it would be reckless to release it on the world prematurely."

The British style:
"Jones is one of my PhD students. For a PhD student, his work is quite good. Indeed, I would even say it compares favourably with the work of some of my other PhD students."

Clearly, this is a very stereotyped picture of the US vs British style, but while exaggerated it does highlight that in the US people tend to use far more superlatives than they do in the UK. In my opinion (but bear in mind that I am British too!), the British approach is certainly more credible. Ideally, you would want to dose the British approach with 10-15% US enthusiasm.

For the full version see: https://www.facebook.com/jonathan.birch.75054/posts/10102039433690700

I also recommend Googling Jonathan Birch, finding his university home page at the LSE ((lse.ac.uk) and checking out his:

- 'About' section
- third person bio
- full CV

They are all extremely well written and if you are an academic you could use them as models.

10.14 More examples of typical things mentioned in a reference letter

Writing about your own or someone else's qualities and soft skills is not easy. Below are a few examples to give you some idea of the kinds of things that can be written about these skills. The examples also highlight the many areas that a reference letter can potentially cover.

HOW REFEREE KNOWS THE CANDIDATE

I have known Valentina Putin since November 2028 when she joined our organisation, and have always found her a most pleasant and trustworthy person to work with. She has a friendly and outgoing personality and is capable of flashes of brilliance in her work.

DESCRIPTION OF CANDIDATE'S RESPONSIBILITIES

From late 2029 Ms Bloggs was involved in coordinating project development and was appointed Projects Manager in Feb 2031 to oversee work projects involving over 150 people. The Project Management duties were as diverse as the projects themselves, which varied from Community Theatre, Visual Arts Displays and Electronic Workshops. Managerial control and operations involved personnel activities, budgetary and financial administration, research and development ...

RELATIONSHIP BETWEEN REFEREE AND CANDIDATE

As a foreign PhD student with unusually good spoken English and communication skills, he quickly established an excellent relationship with the members of my small research group and of my department. He was effective when I asked him to tutor undergraduate students, and showed from the very beginning a great deal of independence, good understanding of the subject as well as initiative and critical thinking (in fact, I even had heated discussions with him in a few occasions, when I was expressing different ideas on how to proceed with the experiments or what to write in the papers; I should mention that in the end he often turned out to be right!).

HOW WELL CANDIDATE WORKS IN A TEAM

Her excellent teamworking attitude allowed her to collaborate effectively with other researchers and to quickly pick up the essentials of new characterization techniques. With clear targets and good motivation she can be a highly dedicated worker.

CANDIDATE'S PERSONALITY

As a Projects Manager, Herman showed himself to be a reliable and hardworking person with a capacity for original ideas as well as close attention to details. He is good at organising work and got on well with people around him. He proved capable of working to tight schedules and maintained a good control over the Project Finances.

10.14 More examples of typical things mentioned in a reference letter (cont.)

CANDIDATE'S HEALTH RECORD

During the period of her employment, I have known her to be very resilient and healthy individual. There is nothing in her health record to prove otherwise.

CANDIDATE'S OUTSTANDING SKILLS

Gojko's role in both projects during the design and implementation phases was absolutely fundamental in making them successful. His extraordinary ability in working out both management and design problems as the projects developed was immediately clear to all the participants.

HOW SUITED THE CANDIDATE IS FOR THE JOB APPLIED FOR IN INDUSTRY

From the duties and responsibilities detailed in your job description I can closely identify Ms Yamashta's abilities and potential to be relevant the requirements. She has an analytical mind and strength of character to meet the demands of such as a post.

HOW SUITED THE CANDIDATE IS FOR THE JOB APPLIED FOR IN RESEARCH

Dr. Veena Huria is ideally suited for this grant. She was a visiting scientist in my laboratory for the period of June 15 to August 15, 2099. During this first visit, the work accomplished by Dr. Huria was very impressive, and her attitude toward her work was both proactive and refreshing. Four publications in international journals have resulted from work: two published and two in preparation.

FOUR EXAMPLES OF CONCLUDING SENTENCES

I can wholeheartedly recommend Ms Kanjika. She is a very willing person and I have no doubt that she will be an asset to your organisation.

Vladimir has my full support in his application to you and I am of the opinion that his considerable potential will be an asset in your company.

In conclusion, I can highly recommend Hao Pei Lin not only on a professional level, but also on a personal level. She is, in my opinion, very professional as well as being an outstanding sales person.

Such is my appreciation of Fernando's work and skills that I would very warmly recommend him for the position he is seeking in your company.

10.15 How can I get and exploit recommendations on LinkedIn?

Recommendations are the LinkedIn equivalent of a reference letter. They serve the same purpose: they provide an objective evaluation of your experience and skills.

As with a reference letter, you can:

- ask people to write recommendations for you, for example when you have completed a particular project or provided someone with a service
- write your own recommendations and get people to post them on your profile

The main differences from a reference letter are that recommendations:

- are an integral part of your profile (in a CV only the referee is mentioned, the reference letter is a separate document)
- will be scanned by search engines, and thus they should contain your key words
- may be spontaneously offered by past and present colleagues, bosses, and customers

If someone spontaneously writes you a recommendation, you will be automatically asked to authorize the publication of this recommendation. Before you make the authorization, check that the recommendation:

- is written in clear, concise and correct English
- contains key words
- is accurate and factual

You can then ask the person to make any changes that you feel would be appropriate. Remember that your recommendations reflect on you: even if the recommendation is very positive in terms of content, if this content is not presented well it could have a negative impact on your image.

10.16   References and reference letters: Do's and Don'ts

➢ Have a separate section for references at the bottom of your CV, or if you have no space mention them in your cover letter.

➢ Do not write 'references available upon request' - it is unnecessary.

➢ Collect reference letters for every job or project that you work on.

➢ Do not write the details of your reference person without their permission.

➢ A reference letter increases your credibility as a suitable candidate as it is written by a (presumably) objective third party who has had direct experience of working with you and who can substantiate both your technical and soft skills.

➢ Do not write the letters yourself without getting the referee's approval / modification.

➢ The letter must be perfectly written both in terms of content, organization and English.

➢ Typical structure: 1) heading 2) positive opening sentence 3) referee's job 4) referee's relation to you 5) details of your qualifications 6) description of your personality 7) positive conclusion.

➢ Do not only include positive information. To make it more credible the letter can include negative information about you, but the emphasis should always be on the positive.

➢ Do not use indentations. Use a simple layout with everything aligned to the left.

➢ Print on good quality paper.

Chapter 11
Cover Letters

Factoids

❖ Searching for "how to write a cover letter" on Google gets around 30 million returns, but only 2.1 million on both Yahoo and Bing.

❖ Amazon returns over 200 books with *CV / resume* in their title.

❖ In a survey of over 300 employers, REED, one of the UK's biggest employment agencies, found that 4 out of 10 recruiters would disregard a job applications without a cover.

❖ The same survey found that in order to maximize the impact of a cover letter, it should be tailored it to the position in question. Even if a candidate has not been specifically asked to include a cover letter, for at least 40% of recruiters it could prove to be the difference.

❖ The experts at REED recommend that before sending a cover letter a candidate should find the answers to the following questions: What does the company do? Who are their competitors? Who are their target audience? What does the role advertised involve? What are essential skills are required?

❖ Experts tend to agree that the maximum length of a cover letter should be one A4 page, but preferably half a page.

❖ A cover letter should be addressed to the person dealing with the applications. If this person is not stated in the job advertisement then experts recommend telephoning to find out the name.

❖ Cover letters are less common in China and Japan than in the west.

© Springer Nature Switzerland AG 2019
A. Wallwork, *English for Academic CVs, Resumes, and Online Profiles*,
English for Academic Research, https://doi.org/10.1007/978-3-030-11090-1_11

11.1 What's the buzz?

A) Look at these typical phrases from cover letters.

- In which paragraph (introductory, middle, final) would they fit best?
- Which phrases would you yourself (not) use? Why? Is there a danger of using standard phrases or using templates?

	intro	middle	final
a) I also have extensive experience in x, which, I believe, would be an ideal match for this position.			
b) I believe that my combination of skills in X, Y and Z, would serve your company well in this position.			
c) I look forward to hearing from you as soon as possible to arrange a time for an interview.			
d) I was interested to read about this opening as I have the qualifications you are seeking. I have several years of experience in X.			
e) I will call to schedule an interview at a mutually convenient time and I look forward to discussing the position with you in more detail.			
f) In addition to my extensive experience in X, I have excellent communication skills.			
g) Of particular note for you and the members of your team to consider are my strong accomplishments in X, Y and Z.			
h) Please accept the attached CV for the position of X as recently advertised in Y.			
i) I am writing with reference to the position you have open for ...			
j) Thank you for your consideration.			

B) What do you think might be the problems with the following extracts from cover letters?

EXTRACT 1

Dear Sandra Jones

My proven track record of successfully performing complex analyses on various corporations makes me an ideal candidate for ...

EXTRACT 2

My broad experience and range of skills make me a superior candidate for this position.

I also have a wide breadth of invaluable experience of the type that gives you the versatility to place me in a number of contexts with confidence that the level of excellence you expect will be met. ...

EXTRACT 3

In addition to my extensive office experience, I have excellent communication skills. I always maintain a mature, gracious and professional manner when communicating with people, even when difficulties arise.

C) Imagine you are applying for your own job, or your boss's job. Write a cover letter that you could send with your CV in order to apply for a job. Alternatively, choose one of the following jobs.

- Marketing assistant for sports car company
- Researcher for international food company
- Programmer for IT department of travel company

This chapter answers two basic questions: *What is a cover letter? How important is it?* It describes how to write a cover letter for a position a) in academia b) in business c) for a position that has not been advertised. The chapter highlights the importance of keeping the letter short and of bearing in mind the impression that the cover letter will create on the reader (e.g. the hiring manager).

11.2   What is a cover letter? How important is it?

A cover letter is the letter that you send along with your CV to a potential employer. A cover letter can be a printed document or an email.

The main aim of a cover letter is to convince the reader to look at your CV. You can do this by giving the HR person the impression that by hiring you their company will improve its efficiency, production and sales, or that you will contribute unique knowledge to a research group.

There is a chance that the recruiter will not even read your cover letter or they may read it after the CV.

However, if they do read the letter first and they don't like what they read, they probably won't look at your CV. Thus, the cover letter is extremely important.

When you are applying for a job online, you may not need to write a cover letter.

11.3   What does the reader (HR person, secretary, professor) expect to find in a cover letter?

If you are sending your cover letter via email, then the subject line of the email should include:

1. the position you are applying for

2. where you saw the advertisement (put this information in brackets)

Examples:

Application for post-doc researcher (LinkedIn)

Internship in Prof Smith's Lab (ad on your website, 7 Mar 13)

The reason for you putting where you saw the job advertised is purely for the company's own internal statistics. It helps them to decide the best location for their adverts.

From the letter itself the reader wants to know:

- what job you are applying for (and perhaps where you saw the advertisement); alternatively, who gave you their name
- why you are interested in this field / company
- how your skills and experience directly apply to the advertised job
- the benefits for the company / institute of employing you
- that you know something about the institute / company
- how you might fit in both in terms of your skills and your personality

The recruiter wants to receive this information as fast and as easily as possible. This means that your letter should be well laid out and organized, and should be short and concise.

11.4 What is the typical structure of a cover letter?

Your letter can be organized as follows:

- say what position you want (and where you saw the job advertised) - it must be clear why you are contacting them
- say what you're doing now, and when your current position will end: provide a very brief selected past history that will interest the reader and give you credibility - your aim is to highlight why you are suitable
- show that you know about the company or research team and highlight the benefit for them of having you in their team - make it clear what you can do for the company
- brief ending – further details can be given in the next email. Many CV / resume experts, particularly in North America, recommend using an assertive ending in which you state that you will be telephoning to arrange an interview. They claim that this will show initiative. I disagree. I see no benefit of doing this - it is the company's prerogative to suggest an interview, not yours
- salutation - *Best regards*

11.5 How should I write a letter for a position in academia?

Below is an example:

> I am writing to inquire about the possibility of a postdoctoral position in your laboratory.
>
> I graduated in 2030 with an MSc in X. I am currently a PhD student in Prof Y's laboratory at the University of Z and I plan to graduate in June 2033. My PhD work has focused on xyz. All my work to date has been published in articles in top international journals. I have also presented my research at several international conferences and have taught two undergraduate classes.
>
> I have experience in:
>
> - x
> - y
> - z
>
> I know that you are currently working on yyy, and I believe that my experience in this area (three EU-funded projects) would be an asset to your team.
>
> I look forward to hearing from you.

What the above letter highlights is that the candidate:

- is writing from the reader's perspective rather than her own perspective. This is clear from the fact that she doesn't stress what she wants and how it would benefit her, but rather how her experience might benefit the research team
- shows that she has various soft skills that are essential for the position, i.e. she can write reports, she can teach (and thus should have good communication skills), and she can give presentations
- believes she has the right technical skills for the job
- is familiar with the team and their work
- can express herself clearly and concisely

11.6 How should I write a letter for a position in business?

Below is an example of how to apply for a position in business or industry. It also shows a possible layout.

Their address

Date

Application for *name of position of job (this line all in bold)*

Dear *name of person (find out HR from website or ring the company – show that you have initiative)*

I saw your advert for a XYZ on your website / in The Times newspaper / in ABC Journal.

[Alternatively, if you have been given the name of the HR person by a mutual third party then you can write: Patrizia Ravenna, who works in your sales department, has told me that you have a position available as a ...]

I think I would be qualified for this position because / I think I may have the qualifications you are looking for because:

- a
- b
- c

I would particularly like to work for IBM because ... / The skills I think I could bring to IBM are: *Write any additional things that you have not written in a, b, c above. The idea is to show that you know about the company (IBM) and that you would fit in perfectly with them*

I am attaching my CV along with references from various professors and previous employers.

I would be available for interview from June 20 (when I finish my current researcher contract at the University of ...)

I look forward to hearing from you.

legible signature

John Smith

A note on punctuation.

After the name of the person you are writing to you can punctuate in one of the following ways:

Dear Adrian Wallwork [*no punctuation*]

Dear Adrian Wallwork: [*a colon, typical of North America*]

Dear Adrian Wallwork, [*a comma*]

Whichever of the above you use, the first word of the following sentence will begin with a capital letter. For example,

Dear Adrian Wallwork,

Your name was given to me by Professor Bond, who thought you might be ...

11.7 How should I apply for job that has not been advertised?

You cannot assume that just because you send someone an email that they will actually open it. No one is under any obligation to respond to an email (or letter), so there is no point in getting frustrated if you receive no reply.

Email subject lines such as the following are not likely to encourage the recipient to open them:

Info on job positions

Do you have any sales positions?

Application for the position of junior developer

Think about why you open certain emails but not others. Generally you open an email when it is clearly for you, for example it comes from someone you know or it is obviously about a work issue that regards you.

You are probably reluctant to open an email from someone you don't know. This could be because you are worried it might contain a virus or simply because you have better things to do.

Faced with this problem, you need to find a way to get your recipient to open your email, even though the recipient has no idea who you are.

Imagine you want a job at ABC. You know someone else who works at ABC, her name is Xun Guan. Your strategy could be:

1) Email Xun Guan and ask her who is the right person to contact at ABC. Xun Guan tells you that Kay Jones is the right person.
2) Email Kay Jones with this subject line:

> Xun Guan: Assistant Marketing Manager position

The idea is that Kay will see Xun Guan's name in the subject line. This will give Kay confidence to open the mail, and she will see that your first line is:

> Dear Kay Jones, Your name was given to me by Xun Guan, who thought you might have a position available for me as an assistant marketing manager.

In any case, Kay may be able to see the beginning of your email without actually opening the email itself (i.e. in the preview pane). This is why the first words of your email are so important, because depending on the effect these words have on the recipient, he / she will decide whether to open your email or not.

Of course, there is a chance that Kay Jones does not even know Xun Guan - the company may be very big. In this case your subject line would be:

> Xun Guan (ABC, marketing dept): Assistant Marketing Manager position

And your first line would be:

> Dear Kay Jones, Your name was given to me by Xun Guan, who works in your marketing department. He thought you might have a position available for me as an assistant marketing manager.

If you were applying for a job in academia, then the strategy is the same (though you would probably exploit your professor's personal contacts first). In this case, contact someone who already works in the research team where you would like a position. Given that the research team is likely to be relatively small compared to a company, you will not need to explain to your recipient who your contact person is. So your subject line and first line of the body of the text could be:

> Xun Guan: Post-doc position in your team

> Dear Professor Gomez, Your name was given to me by Xun Guan. I was wondering whether you might have a position available for ...

11.8   How can I use LinkedIn members when applying for job that has not been advertised and where I do not know anyone in the company / institute?

Finding a job that has not been advertised and is in a company or institute where you do not know anyone is a much more difficult task than those outlined in the previous subsection.

The best solution is probably to telephone the company and institute directly.

If you don't feel confident enough to use the telephone, then you can adopt the following :

First you need to find the name of someone who already works in the company or institute where you would like a job. The best way to do this is through LinkedIn. Go through your contacts to see if anyone in your first-level contacts works in your chosen company. If not, then you need to identify a second-level contact.

The way to find someone is to use LinkedIn's search engine and type in the url of the company or institute. Try to locate someone in your network whose position in the hierarchy is similar to or lower than yours, then you can send an InMail to them. To a first-level contact you can write:

Hi, I am looking for a job in your research team and I was wondering if you could help me. Do you know who would be the best person to contact? Specifically, I am interested in a job in ... Thanks very much for any help you can give me.

To a second-level contact, the text is the same but with a small variation in the first sentence:

Hi, Your name was given to me by a mutual LinkedIn member - Kamran Dehkordi. I am looking for a job ...

11.9   What impression will hiring managers get if I use a template for my own cover letter?

Below is a template for a cover letter intended for a position in business. This template appears on 27 websites offering advice on writing cover letters (I was unable to find the original source). It highlights the dangers of writing a cover letter that is totally generic, i.e. it could have been written by any candidate for practically any business.

Dear Hiring Manager,

I was excited to read about this opening as I have the qualifications you are seeking. I have several years of experience in a wide variety of fields including hi-tech, insurance and the non-profit sector.

Here are some of my skills:

- Verbal and written communications
- Computer proficiency
- Customer service
- Organizing office procedures

In addition to my extensive office experience, I have excellent communication skills. I always maintain a mature, gracious and professional manner when communicating with people, even when difficulties arise.

My broad experience and range of skills make me a superior candidate for this position.

I look forward to hearing from you as soon as possible to arrange a time for an interview.

The problems are:

- the candidate has not taken the trouble to find out the name of the hiring manager
- it is full of generic words, there are only three concrete words *hi-tech, insurance* and *non-profit*
- the skills listed are common to practical anyone who has had some working experience - there is no attempt to show how the candidate is in some way different from the other candidates
- there is no mention of what the candidate knows about the company where he/she is applying for a job
- some parts sound exaggerated and insincere, and thus the candidate loses credibility e.g. the reference to being *excited* and to being a *superior candidate*
- there is an unwarranted presumption that the candidate will be offered an interview

The result is that the hiring manager will be unlikely to read the candidate's CV.

11.10 Using my cover letter, how can I make it look as if I am perfect for the job advertised?

Let's imagine that the advertisement you are responding to contains the following selection criteria.

❑ University degree pertaining to design, implementation and evaluation of environment-related programs and projects

❑ Knowledge of bank operations and institutional issues

❑ Ability to produce high-quality output in response to tight deadlines

❑ Fluent English

A good strategy is to list your skills in the same order (where possible and logical) as in their list of selection criteria. Your letter could be:

> Dear Benedykta Kajilich,
>
> I am very interested in the position of .... advertised in ... on 10 March.
>
> I have a degree in financial ecology and have worked as an intern at the Cooperative Bank in England for three successive summers, which is where I also learned to speak fluent English. During university I have been involved in several projects and managed to complete all of them ahead of schedule.

Not only have you shown that you have the right qualifications, but you have also demonstrated your communication (ability to organize information into a format that matches the reader's expectations) and sales skills (you can sell your own experience).

11.11 What information do I **not** need to include in my cover letter?

The aim of a cover letter is to make key information stand out and to use the least number of words possible. This means that you do not want to include any information that is not strictly necessary.

You do not need to include the following information which is illustrated by the phrases in italics.

1. Your name at beginning e.g. *My name is Nguyen Hung and I ...*

2. Enclosed CV e.g. *Enclosed please find my CV.*

3. Availability for interview e.g. *I am available for interview at any time.*

4. Contact you for additional info e.g. *Please feel free to contact me should you need any further information.*

5. References upon request e.g. *I am happy to provide references on request.*

In a cover letter your name in the main text is irrelevant because it will be in your signature to the letter and also at the top of your CV.

If you are applying for a job you will obviously attach / enclose your CV, so you do not need to mention this fact.

If you really want a job you will always be available for interview, you only need to make reference to the interview if there are times when you absolutely cannot come (in which case you can write: *I will not be available from June 22 to June 29*; you don't need to explain why). If your potential employer is interested in further information about you or wishes to contact your references, they will ask you - you don't need to tell them that you are willing to provide such information, why would you <u>not</u> be willing?

In addition, don't have more than one salutation (*Best regards* is sufficient).

By not mentioning the above five points, you will reduce the length of your cover letter by up to 25%. This will also help to make your key points stand out, as you can see from the example below. By deleting certain phrases the letter below is reduced from 168 words to 116, and from 17 lines to 13. Such deletions could reduce a two-page letter to a more standard one-page letter.

Dear ~~Mrs~~ Helen Murray

~~Application for position of~~ **Post doc DVB researcher**

With reference to the vacancy advertised on your website, I would like to apply for the position of post doc researcher.

~~My name is Tek Saptoka.~~ I am particularly interested in taking active part in the research activities of the Connectivity Systems and Network department. In fact, I spent an internship at XYZ where I also managed a small team of PhD students.

~~As you will note from my CV / resume,~~ In November 2023, I graduated in Telecommunication Engineering at the University of Zulia, Venezuela. For my Masters project, I was an intern at XYZ, where I joined the DVB-TM ad hoc working group and worked on carrier synchronization algorithms for DVB-S2 applications.

~~I am available for interview at any time.~~

~~If you need any further information, do not hesitate to contact me either by phone or e-mail. Enclosed please find my curriculum vitae.~~

I look forward to hearing from you.

~~Yours sincerely,~~

Tek Saptoka

11.12   What are the dangers of writing an email cover letter?

Email is a great way to apply for a job. In many cases an employer will actually request submissions via email rather than traditional mail.

You just have to write the email in the same way as you would write a cover letter to be sent via traditional mail. Both should be written with the same high level of attention.

Unfortunately, many job applicants focus on the informality of emails. They thus write their cover letter quickly without even checking it. Here is a real application for a post-doc position.

> Hi,
>
> I recently completed the PhD in Information Engineering at the University of Pisa, and I'd like to become a good researcher in this field.
>
> I enclose a copy of my curriculum vitae for your consideration.
>
> I would like to increase my experience and knowledge in your laboratories, because they are very technological and .. technology is fundamental to be a good scientist!
>
> I am avalaible for an interview at any time, and I am avalaible for work immediately.

This email would create a terrible impression on the recipient because:

- it clearly took no more than a couple of minutes to write

- it has no structure

- every sentence begins with *I* so it is completely writer focused: *I can, I am, I have, I need, I want*

- there is no mention of any benefit for the recipient's research team

- it contains mainly redundant information

- the writer has tried to be funny (third paragraph)

- the writer has not checked the spelling (*avalaible* should be *available*)

There is absolutely no impression that the candidate is a serious person who understands the importance of good communication skills.

11.13 What should I write if I am simply making an enquiry about a possible job (i.e. no job has actually been advertised)?

Look at your chosen company's website. See what positions there are in the company. Find one that matches your qualifications, and then ask if they have such a position free.

You can begin your letter as follows:

> *I was wondering whether you might have a position available for a software analyst ...*

11.14 My cover letter does not fit on one page, what can I leave out?

Below are some sentences that the candidate of the cover letter in the previous subsection decided to cut.

I combine a sound academic background and a keen interest in issues related to international development with a strong passion and commitment to the pursuit of economic and social justice through the redefinition of the relationship between economics and politics.

Together with the rest of my personal background presented in the enclosed resume, these experiences have helped me develop good social skills and a capacity for reliable and autonomous working habits..

I would be happy to have the opportunity to experience a period of Internship at the CEPR, assisting the staff in those researches that have been indispensable for my studies and from which I tried to learn the admirable working method.

The problem with the above sentences is that add very little value for the reader. They contain very subjective information or information that is difficult to substantiate. As a result they actually detract from the positive impact of the letter.

So when you have finished your letter, make sure you try to eliminate any sentence that does not serve a very clear purpose i.e. any sentence that will not definitely improve your chances of securing an interview.

11.15 What does a good cover look like?

On the next page is an example of a well laid out and constructed cover / motivational letter.

Center for Economic and Policy Research

1611 Connecticut Avenue

NW, Suite 400

Washington, DC 20009

25 November 2030

Full-time Winter International Program Intern January-May 2031

Dear CEPR Staff,

PARAGRAPH 1 I learnt from your newsletter about this interesting opportunity for an intern. In fact, I have read your web pages on a daily basis since I got to know the CEPR from attending Sally Watson's lecture at the *XVIII Encuentro de economistas internacionales sobre problemas de desarrollo y globalización* last March in La Habana, and it has now become an indispensable resource for my understanding of current social and economic problems.

PARAGRAPH 2 I have spent the last academic year at the *Universidad Nacional Autónoma de México (UNAM)* on an Overseas Exchange Student scholarship from the University of Bologna. In the first semester I attended courses of the Maestría en Economía Política and the Maestría en Estudios Latinoamericanos, whereas I spent my second semester doing research for my postgraduate thesis on the perspectives of the regional integration programme *Alternativa Bolivariana para las Américas (ALBA)*.

PARAGRAPH 3 Because of my past experience as head of a cultural association in Bologna I am used to working in a self-directed group and I perform well on both a personal and institutional level. I also have experience in the organization of international events, due to a long collaboration with the University of Groningen in establishing, running and consolidating the European Commenius Course in Bologna.

PARAGRAPH 4 I believe that the combination of my commitment to learning and researching, my long standing interest in Latin American issues, the skills gained from past work experience and the knowledge of CEPR commitments acquired in these months of passionate reading, will enable me to contribute immediately and directly to the CEPR as an International Program Intern.

Thank you for your time and consideration,

Best regards

Below is an analysis of the above cover / motivation letter.

Layout: Everything is aligned to the left, apart from the subject of the letter which is centered and in bold.

Structure: 1) address 2) date 3) subject line 4) opening salutation 5) four paragraphs 6) closing salutation 7) signature 8) reference to the enclosure

Paragraph 1: a) the candidate says where she learned about the position b) she mentions Sally Watson who presumably will be known to the reader c) she shows appreciation for the work that CEPR is doing.

Paragraph 2: Here she shows how what she has studied fits in perfectly with the CEPR's requirements.

Paragraph 3: The candidate states what she can do and then provides strong evidence of it.

Paragraph 4: Again a little pretentious but in reality it makes the candidate sound very sincere, passionate and committed, and in my opinion is a strong ending to her letter.

Below is an example of a longer cover letter / motivational letter.

I would like to apply for a volunteer position for your "New Volunteering @ ToyHouse Project". Please find attached the application form and my CV.

I am 22 years-old, from Pisa (Italy) where I am studying Political Sciences at the University of Pisa. I came to London two years ago, and plan to go back to Italy to finish my degree in June next year.

Currently I'm looking for an opportunity to develop my skills and knowledge in charities and social organizations. The ToyHouse Project appeals to my long-standing interest in childcare and education. In fact, from the age of 15 to 20 I worked as a dance instructor with children from 3 to 12 years of age. It was an amazing working experience that has changed my approach to life and also influenced the choice of my degree. Working with children at such an early age made me really conscious about child labour and how this above all affects developing countries. In addition, during my teenage years I spent I worked at summer camps. My ultimate dream would be to work either in my local community or abroad with NGOs and charities, to help deal with these issues and especially to try to help give these children their childhood back.

I would greatly appreciate the opportunity to be part of your team, and feel sure that your organisation would benefit from my versatile skills. I love spending time with kids and feel that I would be a particularly appropriate person for your Early Years Softplay and Sensory Softplay programs. In addition my fitness training and teaching practice would be appropriate skills for your outdoor Olympic theme program, Hop, Skip & Jump. Furthermore thanks to my experience in the retail sector, I can offer great customer service and help in selecting and stocking toys. Regarding my recent work experience, you will notice from my CV that I have changed jobs quite frequently - each new job has resulted in a higher salary and greater responsibility, and of course, new and useful experiences. I hope you will consider my application because I believe that with my work experience and skills, I would be a positive addition to your team.

I look forward to hearing from you.

Note how the candidate has:

- tried to find the typical things that would be involved in the job and how she would match these needs.

- shown that she is really interested and passionate, and that she has a clear idea of what the job entails. She thus highlights why she is the right person. By doing so she should be able to differentiate herself from all the other applicants.

- mentioned elements from her CV. She has not assumed that the HR person will read her CV in detail

- avoided writing anything that makes it seem that she is exploiting this job opportunity entirely for her own benefit. She makes it look that there will be a clear benefit for her potential employer

11.16 Cover Letters: Do's and Don'ts

➤ From your cover letter the recruiter wants to know:

- o what job you are applying for (and perhaps where you saw the advertisement); alternatively, who gave you their name

- o why you are interested in this field / company

- o how your skills and experience directly apply to the advertised job

- o the benefits for the company / institute of employing you

- o that you know something about the institute / company

- o how you might fit in both in terms of your skills and your personality

➤ Don't use the same cover letter for every job you apply for. Your CV and your cover letter should both look as if they have been written for a specific company or institute. This only entails changing a few details so that your qualifications are a better fit with the requirements of the employer.

➤ Be very careful when 'recycling' a cover letter that you have used previously - ensure you change the address, date, name of person you are writing to, and any references to the company / institute.

➤ Never send a photocopy of your cover letter - each letter you send should be printed separately.

➤ Find documents written by the institute / company and imitate their style, layout (e.g. use of white space), font and font size. Make it seem that you already work for that institute / company!

➤ Do NOT address your recipient in a generic way (e.g. To whom it may concern; Dear Sir / Madam; For the attention of the human resources manager; To the head of the Risk Analysis Department

➤ You can find the name of the professor of the lab you are interested in or the HR person at a company through a third person (e.g. via LinkedIn as outlined in 12.12) or you can telephone the company / institute directly.

➤ Address your recipient by their name. So, find out the name of HR person and address him / her directly e.g. Dear Hugo Smith. The fact that you have taken the trouble to find out the name of the HR person will show that:

you want the job more than the other candidates (you are differentiating yourself from the other candidates who have not made the same effort as you)

you are proactive

> ➢ If you cannot find out the name of the HR person (or other relevant person) then you can write, for example, Attn: Human Resources Manager or Attn: Sales Manager

> ➢ Do not mention anything that:

>> o is not strictly necessary (e.g. your name at the beginning, the fact that you are available for interview and that they can contact you for further information)

>> o could sound arrogant or negative

>> o is very subjective and which you provide no evidence for

>> o makes it sound that the benefit of employing you is solely for you and not for them

> ➢ If you are doing an online job application at a recruiter's website then there may be no opportunity to send a cover letter along with your CV. Also, some employees may ask you not to send a cover letter. This means that some of the information that you would otherwise have put in a cover letter has to be incorporated into your CV. The main missing information is likely to be your demonstration that you have certain soft skills.

> ➢ If you are sending your cover letter via traditional mail, print it on very good quality paper. The quality of the paper reflects on the quality of you as a candidate.

Chapter 12
Checking your English and more ...

Factoids

❖ Research in the UK found that the top 10 things to avoid doing in a CV were related to: bad grammar, spelling mistakes, poor formatting, CVs longer than two pages, casual tone, unusual font style or size, exam grades listed in full, generic interests listed such as cooking or reading, lack of activities related to personal development.

❖ Lewis, a public relations and marketing company, analysed more than 1,000 applications from undergraduates and graduates in the UK seeking trainee positions. More than 90% of applicants had disqualified themselves before the end of the first page of the CV - their CVs were full of errors of spelling and grammar.

❖ Punctuation can change the meaning of a sentence. One UK graduate put under the Interests section: *cooking dogs and interesting people.*

❖ Research by jobs search engine Adzuna found that 1-3 jobseekers jeopardize their chances of getting a job interview by making a spelling mistake in their CV. Of those containing errors, 54% had just one spelling mistake, but 46% contained two or more typos.

❖ The top ten most misspelled English words by native speakers in the UK on their CVs are: 1) *responsibility* 2) *liaise* 3) *university* 4) *experience* 5) *speciality* 6) *communication* 7) *achievement* 8) *management* 9) *environment* 10) *successful.*

❖ Over 50% of recruiters in the UK highlighted poor spelling and grammar as their number one reason for turning down a job application.

❖ Typical grammar and vocabulary mistakes that native speakers make in their CVs include confusing the following: *its / it's; e.g. / i.e.; your / you're; there / they're / their;; to/too; affect / effect; loose / lose; led / lead, advice / advise.*

❖ English has around 205 ways to spell 44 sounds. Around 60% of the 7,000 most common English words have one or more unpredictably used letters - just think of English numbers - *one (won), two (too, to), four (for), six (sicks),* and *eight (ate).* There are around 450 homophones, words that are spelt differently but pronounced the same (*allowed / aloud, blue / blew, sale / sail*) - they can even come in threes (*cite / sight / site, ware / wear / where*).

© Springer Nature Switzerland AG 2019
A. Wallwork, *English for Academic CVs, Resumes, and Online Profiles,*
English for Academic Research, https://doi.org/10.1007/978-3-030-11090-1_12

12.1   What's the buzz?

A) Choose ONE of the verses in the poem below and rewrite it with the correct spelling.

Eye halve a spelling chequer

It came with my pea sea

It plainly marques four my revue

Miss steaks eye kin knot sea.

Eye strike a key and type a word

And weight four it two say

Weather eye am wrong oar write

It shows me strait a weigh.

As soon as a mist ache is maid

It nose bee fore two long

And eye can put the error rite

Its rarely ever wrong.

Eye have run this poem threw it

I am shore your pleased two no

Its letter perfect in it's weigh

My chequer tolled me sew.

B) See how many typos you can find in the following email:

> *Tanks for your male, it was nice to here form you. I was glad to no that you are steel whit the Instituted of Engineering and that they still sue that tool that I made for them, do they need any spare prats for it? I am filling quite tried, tough fortunately tomorrow I'm going a way for tow weeks—I have reversed a residents in the Bahamas!*
>
> *That's all fro now, sea you soon.*

12.1   What's the buzz? (cont.)

C) To see if you English grammar and spelling are better than the average native
    English speaker, read the article on this page: https://www.theguardian.com/
    careers/cv-mistakes and do the exercise entitled "How do you rate your gram-
    matical prowess?"

The key message of this chapter is that your CV / resume is one of the most important
documents that you will ever write. Therefore it is crucial that the English is as
perfect as possible. Spelling, grammar, and translation are focused on as well as the
final checks that should be made before you send your CV (and cover letter). The
chapter also answers the questions: *How should I label my CV file? If they contact
me for an interview, what should I write back? What should I do if I receive a
rejection letter?*

12.2 How important are my CV, cover letter and other such documents?

Incredibly important.

Some written documents can change the course of your career.

CVs, reference letters, cover letters and LinkedIn profiles are examples of such life-changing documents.

So it is certainly worth paying a professional or at least a native English speaker to correct these three documents. The expense should be minimal, you are only submitting about four pages of text.

However, the benefit is massive.

If your documents contain mistakes in the English this will be a bad reflection on you (particularly if in the Language Skills section of your CV you claim to have advanced or fluent English).

12.3 How important is the reader's first impression?

What impression do you think an HR person would have of these beginnings of two cover letters?

1) I know about Your job position and I would like to give my effort to your company, welcoming the opportunity to utilise the knwoledge and experience I have gained ...

2) My name is Nerveena Popovic and I would like to become part in a dynamic and innovative field. I am looking for a stimulating and strongly international atmosphere that favors my career development.

The problems are:

- both candidates have written the letter from their own point of view, i.e. what they want rather than what they can offer the company

- the first candidate has made two errors in his English. He has written *your* with a capital letter. It is not a convention in English to capitalize letters to show respect to the reader. He has also spelt *knowledge* incorrectly. This indicates that he has not taken the time to check his letter, which indicates i) that he is unreliable, ii) that he has totally underestimated the importance of the letter

- the second candidate has begun with her name. Your name will be in your signature, so avoid repeating the same information - keep your letter as short and concise as possible.

These would probably be enough to make the recipient stop reading the letter, with the result that the candidate's CV will probably not even be looked at.

First impressions are massively important. If the initial impact is not 100% positive, you have probably lost your opportunity.

12.4 Am I likely to be a good judge of how accurate, appropriate and effective my CV and cover letter are?

No, you are not - even if you are a native speaker of English.

Quickly skim the cover letter below. On a scale of 0-3, how would you assess the following five factors in the cover letter below?

- English grammar
- English vocabulary
- English expressions
- Structure of the letter
- Relevance of the content

In last decade Nano science and Nanotechnology has been playing a big role in Research and Industrial development. IPR has put the multiplier effect on the scientific and industrial development for socio-economic benefits. IPR reserves the rights of scientific person, industrialist, R&D organization and a common man for their intellectuality, novelty *etc.* From this given background it is clear that I hold keen interest in IPR and thus would like to gain deep knowledge of IPR and its economic effect. It is understood fact that legal expert and scientific personnel are facing lots of problem to design or implement IP issues for Nano science and Nanotechnology work. In this regards I want to explore my skill to get the theoretical as well as practical knowledge.

During my IPR Diploma course, I have found that I am decently skilled in the art of persuasion, as my teachers and my colleague will rightly testify. I've had a knack of getting my point across very well, communicating with people, understanding their needs and providing them with a value proposition which is truly hard to refuse. My skills lie in my ability to comprehensively read and understand the situation and act quickly and yet smartly. But of what use is a raw skill, unless it is sharpened? So to this end, I decided to apply for intensive Summer Course on Intellectual Property and Business Entrepreneurship in IPR at this prestigious organization so as to help me understand more about IPR, to help me understand the mind of the consumer better and to learn some soft skills which have proven to be effective over many years. And laden with textbook knowledge, I wish to implement the skills that I have learned in the real world. I want to prove to myself that I have truly been benefited by this education and what better place to start, than an institution as reputed as yours? For your kind perusal I have enclosed by resume. Deep hope of your encouraging response. Thanks you so much in advance, ***please consider my application for WIPO scholarships scheme.***

12.4 Am I likely to be a good judge of how accurate, appropriate and effective my CV and cover letter are? (cont.)

Unfortunately a recruiter would probably give this candidate a rating of 0 or 1, for each of the items. The English is a strange combination of sentences that could have been written by a native speaker alongside bad mistakes, a mix of colloquial and very formal expressions, and expressions that probably exist in the applicant's native language but do not exist in English e.g. *Deep hope of your encouraging response.*

The structure is not conventional. The candidate ends by mentioning the reason for his letter (an application for a scholarship) - this is key information and should be at the beginning. He has highlighted this information by using bold italics, but in reality it would have been better to place it on a separate line at the top of the letter. On the other hand, the beginning reads like an introduction to a scientific paper on the topic of IPR, a topic that presumably the reader will be well acquainted with.

However, the writer was pleased with his letter. He had no idea that it was not a good cover letter. It requires an expert to judge whether your letter is good enough, and I repeat again, it is worth paying someone to revise such an important document.

12.5   How important is my English?

I once received a CV from a non-native teacher of English who wanted to work for me. In the Work Experience section, she wrote that she *teached English at all levels.* To me this indicated that the teacher was incompetent on two levels. She demonstrated that i) she did not have a good command of English, ii) she had not taken the trouble to spell check her CV (given that *teached* is a word that does not exist, a spell checker would have highlighted it).

12.6   How important is spelling in English?

Much more than in most other languages.

On June 15, 1992, Don Quayle, the then vice President of the USA, was attending a spelling bee (a competition to see which student could spell the best) at an elementary school in New Jersey. Quayle went up to the blackboard and altered 12-year-old student William Figueroa's correct spelling of *potato* to *potatoe.* Quayle was widely lambasted for his error which has been immortalized on YouTube.

English spelling is a major problem for native speakers. Here are some words that mother tongue adults often have difficulty with: *appropriate, character, conscientious, eliminate, embarrass, forty, liaison, maintenance, marriage, necessary, opportunity, rhythm, tomorrow, transferred.* Spelling mistakes are also made by native speakers, for example: *catagory* (instead of the correct spelling: category), *definately* (definitely), *equiptment* (equipment), *foriegn* (foreign), *fullfill* (fulfill), *goverment* (government), *maintainence* (maintenance), *neccessary* (necessary), *relevent* (relevant), and *transfered* (transferred). Native speakers also frequently confuse *they're, there,* and *their; its* and *it's.*

As a consequence of English spelling being difficult, bad spelling in the Anglosphere is associated with a poor education and lack of intelligence. In addition, a spelling mistake or other typo indicates to the reader that you didn't take time to check your CV or letter, and if you didn't take the time to do that, then in your professional life this may indicate that you don't take time to check your work or your data - not a good sign for a potential employer.

12.7   Can I use Google Translate to translate my CV and LinkedIn profile?

You can use Google Translate or other such software to provide the first draft, but afterwards you will need to do a lot of work on it. To learn how to use Google Translate, see Chapter 5 of my book *English for Academic Correspondence* published by Springer.

12.8 What do I need to be careful about when translating from my language into English?

The typical phrases used when writing CVs, letters and emails vary massively from one country to another. This means you need to be very careful when translating such phrases from your own language into English.

For example, the typical ending of a cover letter in your language may be *Waiting for your favorable response* or *I remain in expectation of your rapid reply* but in English these phrases do not exist. Many such phrases are formalities and add no real content to the letter, so the simplest solution is to delete them.

However, a salutation at the beginning and end of a letter or email is normally required. The solution is to use phrases that you are 100% certain exist in English. So in this case the simplest solution is to use *Dear + first name + family name* at the beginning, *and Best regards* at the end. If you adopt this policy, you will not make mistakes. If you are creative or write too much, then you will probably make many mistakes.

You also have to be clear in your mind what information a recruiter will and will not find relevant. For example, in some countries when you graduate from university as a lawyer, accountant, engineer, architect etc, you have to pass an additional state exam which then authorizes you to practice professionally in your chosen field. However, if you are applying for a job outside your own country, providing such information is not only irrelevant but also potentially confusing to people in those countries where such state exams do not operate.

12.9   Will I create a good impression if I use sophisticated grammar and complex sentence constructions?

No.

Look at the example below.

> It is with your organization that I desire to offer marketing, contract administration and project management experience. Having a strong background utilizing a variety of design standards along with proposal requirements, I am certain that my skills and experience, when linked with the vision of your company, will serve to create dramatic, profitable results.

The writer of the example above evidently thought she was going to impress the HR manager with her command of English. But in reality the sentences do not sound natural. Due to their length, they are also hard to read and absorb.

So, as in everything you write, use short sentences in clear English. Your aim is make it easy for the reader to absorb the information you are presenting. The HR manager's impression of the candidate above would be of someone who cannot express herself simply and who is rather insincere.

In addition, don't try to be clever and don't philosophize.

> I'm keen on sports, travelling, arts, especially painting, poetry and music. These are definitely ones of the most impacting aspects on our life, as likely they are incorruptible elements of knowledge to be forwarded to the next generations.

The problems with the above paragraph are:

- his hobbies and interests should be listed in his CV not in a cover letter

- the HR person is not interested in the candidate's opinion of the role of art

- he has tried to show that his interest in art is important, but in doing so he has to use quite complicated concepts and this leads to mistakes. For example, the expressions *impacting aspects* and *incorruptible elements of knowledge* do not exist, and *forwarded* should be *handed down*

12.10 What final checks should I make before sending my CV / resume and the cover letter?

Before you send any important document, ask a friend or colleague to check through your final version.

Then:

- check for consistency: have you always used bold, italics and initial capitalization for the same purpose? is your grammar consistent (e.g. when describing your roles have you also used the same grammatical form - *developed* three applications for xyz, *wrote* technical documentation for pqr; rather than a mixture - *developing* three applications for xyz, *wrote* technical documentation for pqr;

- do a very final spelling check. HR people are capable of rejecting candidates simply on the basis that the CV or letter contained one single spelling mistake. Make sure you check the spelling of any names of software, products, institutions, companies etc (i.e. words that an automatic spell checker will not find). Also check for misspellings such as *form* instead of *from*, or *addiction* rather than *addition* i.e. spelling mistakes that an automatic checker cannot find.

12.11 On LinkedIn what final checks do I need to make?

Paste your profile in a Word file and use the spell checker to ensure that you have not made any spelling mistakes.

Just one spelling mistake is enough for your CV to be rejected. Likewise, a recruiter will not impressed if they find spelling mistakes in your LinkedIn profile.

Finally, get friends and colleagues to assess the profile for you and to give you critical feedback.

12.12 If they contact me for an interview, what should I write back?

Below is a typical email that you might receive from an HR department.

> Thank you for sending us your CV. We would like to invite you for an interview on 10 March at 10.00. Please could you confirm that this time would be suitable for you.

Your reply could be:

> Thank you for contacting me. I would pleased to come for an interview on 10 March at 10.00.
>
> I very much look forward to meeting you.

If the time is not suitable, then rather than inventing an excuse, you can simply say

> Thank you for contacting me. I am very interested in coming for an interview, but unfortunately I cannot attend on 10 March. Would it be possible either the week before or after? I could come at any time of day to suit you.
>
> I apologize for the inconvenience and I very much look forward to meeting you.

If you think it is necessary to explain why you are unable to come on the suggested day, you could write:

> Thank you for contacting me. I confirm that I am 100% interested in coming for an interview, but unfortunately on that day ...
>
> ... my brother is getting married
>
> ... I will still be in Japan on an assignment for my current company.

12.13 Checking your English and more ... : Do's and Don'ts

➤ Your CV is one of the most important documents that you will write during your life. Consider paying a profession native English proofreader to check it for you.

➤ Do not copy and paste your profile into your cover letter or vice versa.

➤ In an important document - a report, a presentation, a CV - a few spelling mistakes could mean that people don't take you seriously.

➤ Always use a spell checker and never introduce last-minute changes to a document without redoing the spell check. The spell checker will also check whether you have invented any English words or you've left words in your own language.

➤ Spell checkers won't find every word - no spell checker or grammar checker in the world will tell you if you've confused asses (donkeys, idiots) with assess (evaluate). So give your document to someone else to read. If your eyes will only see what you think you have written, a pair of fresh eyes should be able to pick up a lot more errors.

➤ Be consistent - if you're going to use US spelling, then use it throughout your document.

➤ Telephone the institute / company if they have not been in touch within two weeks. Even if were not successful, some HR people will give you a few minutes of valuable feedback that you can integrate into your CV for next time.

➤ Do not create your CV at the last minute and then send it off without double checking anything. In the words of REED employment agency: *A day spent on your CV is better than six months of waiting for a reply.*

➤ Do ensure that you label your CV with your name e.g. Donald Smith CV.

Appendix - Downloadable templates for CVs

Template for a CV

Below is a possible template for a two-page CV.

You can download a Word version of the template from my website: https://e4ac.com/courses-downloads/

Your name should be in 12 pt, headings in 11 pt and the rest in 10 pt. Your name and personal details should be centered if you have no photo, or aligned to the left with your photo on the right.

The parts in [square brackets] are optional. Obviously, you will have more or less subsections in each section depending on your experience.

Instead of an Executive summary, you may just have an Objective.

To learn more about what to include in each section, see the cross-references in brackets below:

1. name (4)

2. personal details (4)

3. objective / personal statement / executive summary (6)

4. education (7)

5. work experience (8)

6. skills (9)

7. personal interests (10)

8. publications (8.9, 8.10)

9. references (11)

© Springer Nature Switzerland AG 2019   183
A. Wallwork, *English for Academic CVs, Resumes, and Online Profiles*,
English for Academic Research, https://doi.org/10.1007/978-3-030-11090-1

184

First Name + Second Name

first.second@email.com; cell phone number

[dd/mm/yyyy; nationality; gender]

Summary

- blah
- blah
- blah
- blah

Work Experience

2026-2032	Name of company + [www.etc]
	Position, role + details of work carried out highlighting technical and soft skills
2025-2026	Name of company + [www.etc]
	Position, role + details of work carried out highlighting technical and soft skills

Education

2016-2022	Name of university / institute + [www.etc]
	Qualification obtained + [further details, highlight technical and soft skills]
2015-2016	Name of university / institute + [www.etc]
	Qualification obtained + [further details, , highlight technical and soft skills]

page 2

Skills

Languages	Language 1: mother tongue; [Other main language: fluent]; English: spoken (proficiency), listening (proficiency), written (proficiency) and reading ((proficiency); [English exams passed: name of exam, grade]
Software	software 1 [level of proficiency]; software 2 [level of proficiency); etc
Technical	technical 1 [level of proficiency]; technical 2 [level of proficiency); etc

Personal interests

Interest 1:	Blah blah blah ...
Interest 2:	Blah blah blah ...
Interest 3:	Blah blah blah ...

Publications

Publication 1

Publication 2 etc

References

Name 1: position; email address; website address

Name 2: position; email address; website address

Name 3: position; email address; website address

Template for a resume

On the next page is a possible template for a one-page resume.

The parts in [square brackets] are optional. Obviously, you will have more or less subsections in each section depending on your experience.

Instead of an Executive Summary (also called Career Highlights), you may just have an Objective.

Note: In addition to the Experience and Education sections, you may also wish to put one or more of the following sections:

- Associate Memberships / Professional Affiliations
- Certifications
- Honors
- Professional Training
- Publications
- Related Experiences
- Skills (technical and language)

Unlike a CV, a resume generally does not include a photo, a Personal Interest section, or a References section.

First Name + Second Name

first.second@email.com; cell phone number

Summary

- blah
- blah
- blah
- blah

Experience

Most recent position

Name of company + [www.etc]; dates of employment

5-6 line description of role including key skills (technical and soft)

Second-most recent position

Name of company + [www.etc]; dates of employment

2-4 line description of role including key skills (technical and soft))

etc

Education

Most recent educational qualification

Name of university / institute + [www.etc]; dates of attendance

Qualification obtained + [further details, highlight technical and soft skills]

Second-most recent educational qualification

etc

Keys to *What's the buzz?* exercises

Chapter 2

1) Related work experience 2) Qualifications and skills 3) Easy to read 4)) Spelling and grammar 5) Education 6) individuality/desire to succeed 7) Clear objective 8) Personal experiences 9) Computer skills

Survey: https://www.kent.ac.uk/careers/cv.htm really useful

Chapter 3

Equal Opportunities legislation in many countries means that you are NOT obliged to include a photo or state your:

- age
- gender
- marital status, children
- race / nationality

Such legislation is extremely important and is designed to make sure that everyone has an equal chance of getting a job.

Of course, with regard to your age, the recruiter will be able to make a good guess of how old you are from the dates of your education on your CV.

Names are a particular case. If your name does not give a clear indication of what sex you are to someone who is not of your nationality, then you could decide either to include a photograph or to state your gender (male or female). This will then avoid any initial embarrassment in a phone call or face-to-face interview, when maybe the recruiter is expecting someone of the opposite sex.

© Springer Nature Switzerland AG 2019
A. Wallwork, *English for Academic CVs, Resumes, and Online Profiles,*
English for Academic Research, https://doi.org/10.1007/978-3-030-11090-1

Alternatively in your cover letter, you could sign yourself, for example:

Mr Andrea Rossi (if you are a man),

Ms Andrea Schmidt (if you are a woman).

Given that your aim is not to waste valuable space on your CV, you do <u>not</u> need to include the following information:

- your traditional postal address (either home or work) - recruiters are only likely to contact you by phone or by email
- names of other members of your family (e.g. your father's name - note: this applies to some African and Asian countries)

You also do <u>not</u> need to include / state:

- your fax number
- Skype, Facebook, Twitter addresses
- whether you have completed your military service
- whether you have a driving license

Chapter 4

A)

According to Tom Jackson in his book *Resume Express*: An accomplishment is a result, contribution, or achievement you are responsible for in a particular job or activity. You have produced accomplishments in every area of your life: past or current jobs, school projects, volunteer work. Accomplishments create a positive picture and are hard to ignore. .... Duties are what your job *required* you to do. Accomplishments are the *tangible results* you produced. Everybody has *duties*, but *accomplishments* are unique.

D)

1) It seems like the seismic threats will impact on private industries. Better:

   A position in a private industry as a technical surveyor of seismic threats.

2) It seems that the candidate wishes to demonstrate *expertise and progress*, whereas *progress* is a verb in this case (not a noun) and relates to *field* and not *expertise*. Better:

   A position offering opportunities to demonstrate expertise, and to progress in the field of drafting specifications for software.

3) In an attempt to be concise and to use the minimum number of words possible, the candidate has written two strings of nouns which make her Objective difficult, if not impossible, to read. The solution is to use more prepositions and verbs:

A challenging position in training for a private industry focusing on developing alternative work styles to enable staff to enhance their careers.

Chapter 5

A) a) 2 *intersted, Shakespear*; 3 *here* (instead of *hear*); 6 *martial* (instead of *marital*); b) 12 (and possibly others) c) 5, 10 d) 4 e) 8, 9, 11

B) The first draft is very generic, she has just made the same point several times. There are vague expressions that could have been written by anyone. Concrete examples are what is needed. For example, there is no mention of the specific film projects she had been involved in, or how she would like to compare French film making styles with English ones. Her unique 'selling' point is that she is French - - for the other students and especially the lecturers the fact that she is French and is familiar with French cinema will be a real bonus.

Chapter 7

The top 10 words to include on an application form are: *Achievement, Active, Developed, Evidence, Experience, Impact, Individual, Involved, Planning, Transferable skills*

The 10 words to avoid: *Always, Awful, Bad, Fault, Hate, Mistake, Never, Nothing, Panic, Problems*

Source: http://money.guardian.co.uk/work/story/0,1456,1589620,00.html

Chapter 8

Not any particular order:

- Ability to put themself in the other person's shoes
- Competent + experience in specific topic
- Confident but not domineering
- Easy to get on with – reliable, sociable, friendly
- Good academic results
- Good communication skills: including being a good listener, communicating clearly and convincingly

- Good language skills
- Good time management and with stress when working towards deadlines
- Problem solver, ability to see the big picture
- Similar but not identical background

Chapter 9

The letter will create a positive impression on the reader because it i) is well organized; ii) gives a clear indication of both Adele's intellectual and technical capacity as well as her personality; iii) begins and ends in a very positive way, thus creating a good impression both at the beginning and the end of the letter.

The letter is structured as follows:

1) writer explains who he/she is + connection to candidate;

2) candidate's academic background;

3) writer's view on his/her relationship with the candidate in terms of the info given in paragraph 2;

4) writer outlines candidate's technical skills + personal skills (the kind of skills that might be more difficult for the candidate to describe herself in her CV);

5) positive ending + offer to provide further info

1. I can assure you that no person would be better for the job [= better to employ no one rather than employ this person].

2. She's an unbelievable worker [= dishonest].

3. Every hour with him was a happy hour [= drunk at work].

4. You would indeed be fortunate to get this person to work for you [= exceptionally lazy].

5. I most enthusiastically recommend this candidate with no qualifications whatsoever [= no diplomas].

6. I would urge you to waste no time in making this candidate an offer of employment [= not worth employing].

7. All in all, I cannot say enough good things about this candidate or recommend her too highly [= not worth employing].

8. She could not care less about the number of hours she has to put in [= rarely at work].

9. There is nothing you can teach a man like him [= unbelievably unintelligent].

Chapter 11

a) Introduction: d, h, j; middle a, f, g; final b, c, e, f. Personally I would avoid c, e, and g, as they sound as if they come from the kind of template that you can find online and may say strange in the middle of other sentences.

B): They all sound quite arrogant and contain statements that are difficult to substantiate. 1) Do not begin your letter in a self-promoting way. 2) Do not use adjectives which are designed to show how fantastic you are, may simply sound insincere or improbable. 3) Don't mention social skills for which you provide no concrete evidence. Never just describe, always demonstrate.

Sources for the Factoids

Chapter 1

Factoids taken from the following websites and books:

https://uk.finance.yahoo.com/news/two-five-people-professional-jobs-uk-unhappy-130551937.html

www.financialexecutives.org/.../CSR_Everything%20you%20needed%20to%20know.ppt -

https://www.reed.co.uk/career-advice/what-recruiters-are-really-looking-for-in-your-cv/

Brilliant answers to tough interview questions, Susan Hodgson, Pearson

Brilliant CVs, Jim Bright & Jonanne Earl

Interview others (Steps to Success) Lorenza Clifford, A & C Black

Winning CVs for first-time job hunters, Kathleen Houston

Chapter 2

1) https://rooting-for-you.cenedella.com/even-a-genius-has-to-sell-himself-the-remarkable-resume-of-leonardo-da-vinci-453fb6d53efd

2) https://www.theguardian.com/small-business-network/2018/jan/22/virtual-reality-and-mr-men-books-companies-reveal-their-unusual-recruitment-tools

3) https://www.theguardian.com/small-business-network/2018/jan/22/virtual-reality-and-mr-men-books-companies-reveal-their-unusual-recruitment-tools

4) https://www.inc.com/michael-schneider/its-harder-to-get-into-google-than-harvard.html

5) Author's own data.

© Springer Nature Switzerland AG 2019
A. Wallwork, *English for Academic CVs, Resumes, and Online Profiles*,
English for Academic Research, https://doi.org/10.1007/978-3-030-11090-1

Chapter 3

Author's own data.

Chapter 4

1) https://www.elsevier.com/connect/survey-how-do-you-manage-your-academic-profile

2 and 7) https://www.cv-library.co.uk/career-advice/cv/write-personal-statement-cv-2018/

3, 4 and 6) Wikipedia

5) Matthews, David (7 April 2016). "Do academic social networks share academics' interests?". Times Higher Education. Retrieved 2016-04-22.

Chapter 5

1-6) https://www.thestudentroom.co.uk/showthread.php?t=2878535

7) https://www.buzzfeed.com/sophiegadd/pls-let-me-go-to-your-uni?utm_term=.pbydwly02b#.hmnV0XDrl7

8-9) https://www.whatuni.com/advice/applying-to-uni/the-most-ridiculous-things-ever-put-on-a-uni-application/58250/

10-12 https://www.studenthut.com/articles/11-things-not-put-your-personal-statement

Chapter 6

Apart from the Japan and UK facts, all the other facts originally appeared in my book *English for Presentations at International Conferences*. They were taken from info provided by my PhD students.

Japan: https://www.theguardian.com/world/2018/aug/08/tokyo-medical-school-admits-changing-results-to-exclude-women

UK: https://www.theguardian.com/education/2018/aug/10/scientists-launch-campaign-to-overturn-gender-stereotypes

Chapter 7

1) https://www.theguardian.com/careers/careers-blog/lie-degree-cv-jobseekers-graduate

2) https://www.telegraph.co.uk/finance/jobs/10614757/Employers-at-risk-of-fraud-from-foreign-jobseekers-CV-lies.html

3-7) Originally appeared in my book *English for Academic Correspondence*.

8) Author's own data.

Chapter 8

1 and 7) *English for Interacting on Campus*, SpringerNature

2) https://www.quora.com/What-is-the-hardest-language-to-learn-for-English-speakers

3 and 4) http://www.nationalsoftskills.org/the-soft-skills-disconnect/

5) https://business.financialpost.com/executive/careers/the-biggest-predictor-of-career-success-not-skills-or-education-but-emotional-intelligence

6) https://www.reed.co.uk/career-advice/what-words-should-i-use-on-my-cv/

Chapter 9

1) https://it.businessinsider.com/hobbies-look-great-on-resume-2017-2/?r=US&IR=T

2 and 3) https://www.resumecoach.com/write-a-resume/personal-interests/#should-you-include-your-hobbies-on-a-resume

4-9) These factoids originally appeared in my book *English for Academic Correspondence*.

Source of quotes in *What's the Buzz*:

https://www.reed.co.uk/career-advice/what-recruiters-are-really-looking-for-in-your-cv/

Suzanne Moore, Guardian columnist - https://www.theguardian.com/money/2018/jun/19/how-to-write-the-perfect-cv-first-refuse-to-play-this-stupid-game?CMP=Share_iOSApp_ Other

https://www.theguardian.com/small-business-network/2018/jan/22/virtual-reality-and-mr-men-books-companies-reveal-their-unusual-recruitment-tools

Lyn Tyler, managing director of Bagelman - https://www.theguardian.com/small-business-network/2018/jan/22/virtual-reality-and-mr-men-books-companies-reveal-their-unusual-recruitment-tools

Chapter 10

http://www.ling.upenn.edu/~beatrice/humor/ambiguous-recommendations.html

Chapter 11

1, 2 and 8) Author's own data

3-7) https://www.reed.co.uk/career-advice/what-recruiters-are-really-looking-for-in-your-cv/

Chapter 12

1) https://www.independent.co.uk/news/uk/home-news/employers-sifting-through-applications-likened-to-swiping-through-tinder-as-research-shows-people-9988512.html

2) https://www.thecvstore.net/blog/cv-spelling-mistakes/

3) https://www.theguardian.com/money/2018/jun/19/how-to-write-the-perfect-cv-first-refuse-to-play-this-stupid-game?CMP=Share_iOSApp_Other

4 and 5) https://www.telegraph.co.uk/finance/jobs/11498666/top-ten-spelling-mistakes-job-seekers-employees-cvs-curriculum-vitae.html

6) https://www.reed.co.uk/career-advice/what-recruiters-are-really-looking-for-in-your-cv/

Index

© Springer Nature Switzerland AG 2019
A. Wallwork, *English for Academic CVs, Resumes, and Online Profiles*,
English for Academic Research, https://doi.org/10.1007/978-3-030-11090-1

Printed in the United States
By Bookmasters

Helen MacInnes

A Fawcett Crest Book
Fawcett Publications, Inc., Greenwich, Conn.